Additional Praise for
Getting an Investing Game Plan

"I have known Vern Hayden for many years and have greatly respected him as a person and a financial planner. I believe Vern's book is very important for it will allow a great number of readers to access his thinking and advice, which up to now were available primarily to his personal clients. Read, enjoy, and benefit."

> —William L. Anthes, Ph.D.
> President and CEO
> National Endowment for Financial Education

"Before you invest you need to follow Vern's ten steps to building a successful investment strategy. It is a simple, easy-to-understand process by one of the pioneers of financial planning."

> —Miles Gordon
> Former CEO of ING Advisors Network and
> Chairman of the board of the Financial Network
> Investment Corporation

"Vern Hayden is a thoughtful investment advisor and he brings a complex subject into clear focus. This book is full of useful, relevant, and understandable information for anyone's investment game plan."

> —Eileen M. Sharkey, CFP
> Sharkey, Howes & Javer Inc.

GETTING AN INVESTING GAME PLAN

Creating It, Working It, Winning It

**Vern C. Hayden, CFP
with Maura Webber
and Jamie Heller**

WILEY

John Wiley & Sons, Inc.

Published by John Wiley & Sons, Inc., Hoboken, New Jersey.
Published simultaneously in Canada.

For general information on our other products and services, or technical support, please contact our Customer Care Department within the United States at 800-762-2974, outside the United States at 317-572-3993 or fax 317-572-4002.

Wiley also publishes its books in a variety of electronic formats. Some content that appears in print may not be available in electronic books.

For more information about Wiley products, visit our web site at www.wiley.com.

Library of Congress Cataloging-in-Publication Data:

Hayden, Vern.
    Getting an investing game plan : creating it, working it, winning it / Vern C. Hayden with Maura Webber and Jamie Heller.
      p. cm.
    Includes bibliographical references and index.
    ISBN 0-471-26392-3 (cloth)
    1. Investments.   I. Webber, Maura.   II. Heller, Jamie.   III. Title.

HG4521 .H367   2003
332.6—dc21   2002191065

Printed in the United States of America.

10 9 8 7 6 5 4 3 2 1

To
Ruth Storm Hayden
1909–1998
My mother was a humble, loving, caring, hardworking minister's wife, who, in tandem with her husband, my father, the late Reverend Clarence Hayden, affected the spiritual lives of many people. Her spiritual legacy of kindness and unconditional love left an indelible imprint on all who knew her, especially her grateful son.

Foreword

The investment game has changed over the past two decades. Historically, the challenge facing investors has been to identify good investments. While that's obviously still important, investors increasingly recognize that that alone isn't enough. Five good mutual funds can still make a bad portfolio, or at least one that's inappropriate for a given investor's goals. It's becoming clear that investors must move beyond good versus bad investments and toward appropriate or inappropriate usage of investments, taking into account their time horizons and risk tolerance. It's a level of analysis that doesn't transfer well to the sound-bite world of televised financial advice, but it's where investors need to go if they are to succeed.

In this new reality, investments are the easy part. Determining whether a stock or a fund is a quality offering with reasonable prospects is a fairly straightforward task in these days of widespread financial information. Knowing where a given stock or fund fits in your portfolio—that's a much trickier task. Ultimately, however, the art of investing involves more than simply identifying good investments; it means finding the right match between investment and investor. It's no easy job. Yet it's what good financial planners do every day, and it's the reason that I have such great respect for these people.

When I first started tracking mutual funds in the mid-1980s, I knew of brokers who could sell you stocks or funds, but I knew little about the growing field of financial planning, which aimed to craft full-fledged financial solutions for their clients. Over time, however, I came to know a number of financial advisors and became a part of their discussions. Like most investors, I was thinking in words or phrases, but these advisors were thinking in fully formed paragraphs. They understood, quite correctly, that investments alone were not the full game. To succeed, you need to know how and when to deploy them; you need a game plan.

Vern Hayden is as fine a planner as I know. He's up on all the latest academic research, yet he retains a remarkable ability to translate the often arcane language of finance into straightforward counsel that even beginning investors can understand. Not surprisingly, these traits have made him a favorite guest on CNBC and other financial media. But unlike some media favorites, Vern never opts for the sensational over the sensible. His advice is always on target and always well grounded.

I think you'll find this book valuable. It's full of great ideas and tangible examples that will show you how to craft a sensible investment plan. Whether you continue on your own or opt for the services of a professional advisor to help you manage your money, this book will start you in the right direction with a game plan for the future.

DON PHILLIPS
Managing Director
Morningstar, Inc.

Acknowledgments

Looking back at the undertaking of this book, I'm reminded of my days when I was stationed at Kingsley Field Air Force Base in Oregon. Though the glory often went to the pilots, I was one of the many thousands of ground support people who played a part in getting the planes off the ground. This book is no different. We have a lot of people to thank for the support that they provided to make this book fly.

It wasn't always apparent that it would. For some time I knew I wanted to write a book to help people gain the financial means they needed to live out their dreams. Yet I wasn't sure how to do it. I am ever indebted to all the folks at Wiley who did. I am particularly grateful to Joan O'Neil, Pamela van Giessen, and Bill Falloon. Their belief in me and the project brought my game plan to life.

Bill Falloon had the vision to see the potential in my proposal and the courage to take a chance on a new author. I'll never forget how thrilled I was to hear back from Bill after I'd left a cold call in his voice mail about my book idea. Ever since, Bill's insightful editing and gentle guidance through the intricacies of the publishing process have been invaluable.

Thanks also to Maura Webber, a gifted writer. Through evenings, weekends, and vacations, Maura listened to me explain the nuances of the investment process and helped me craft my thoughts into the meaningful language of a book. I am also thankful to have had the chance to work again with Jamie Heller, who previously hired me to write the *Game Plan* column for TheStreet.com. Jamie's brilliant editorial sense ensured that the ideas and track of the book were meaningfully connected. From the big picture conception of the project through to the final details, Jamie led us to the finish line.

I owe many thanks to my staff. Joan Kokoruda, my secretary, oversaw the logistics of the process, typing endless pages of text while always keeping the troops in sync. Her sense of humor kept us smiling. Gerard Gruber, chief of operations at Hayden Financial, did critical research and fact-checking of the book. His firm grasp of the financial industry and our investment process added depth to the text.

We were privileged to work with numerous talented professionals whose skills and knowledge enhanced the book. Helaine Tishberg, a graphic artist, helped crystallize complex concepts and bring them to life in images. Megan Campion worked tirelessly obtaining permissions. At Wiley, Mary Daniello added polish to our copy and prepared the manuscript for production along with Cape Cod Compositors. Also thanks to Melissa Scuereb and Mary Watson, both of whom always had the answers, or knew how to find them, to 1,001 questions. I also am grateful to Bruce McIntyre, who helped give the book its tone, and to Dennis Watkins and Faith Ann Jenkins.

Thanks also to Don Phillips, Annette Larson, Kathy Habiger, and all the folks at Morningstar. Their talent and voluminous information added immeasurably to the quality of this book. For insight into the financial planning world, Sandra Knisely and Al Hockwalt were immensely helpful. Phyllis Primus organized a significant part of my marketing program. I also owe a special thanks to Dr. William Pite for his critical review of the book through its many stages. His unique perceptions of how investments work and how people relate to their money were always thought-provoking and illuminating.

Before the book was even a concept, there were many people in television and the media who helped me find my public voice. I'll be forever grateful to Berlinda Garnett, the first person to book me on CNBC's *Money Club* with Bill Griffeth. I'm grateful for that first interview and all the ones that have followed. Brenda Buttner, a former CNBC anchor now at the Fox News Channel, has also invited me on as a frequent guest and has included me in numerous special segments and various writings. Thank you, Bill and Brenda.

Many thanks to David Landis, my editor at TheStreet.com, who made my columns look better than I ever could. Thanks to Dean Shepherd for the many television interviews he did with me at NBC and Bloomberg. Special thanks also to Karin Price Mueller, Alison Moore, Gary Schreier, Ann Marie Cocozza, Lori Hoffman, and all the bookers and producers who have been kind enough to put me on the air.

Finally, I am grateful to the team's extended friends, family, and colleagues who have tirelessly supported us throughout our endeavor.

Oksana Makarenko, my life partner, has been a great source of strength. Her love and encouragement made life easier for me during this experience. My daughter, Kirsten Hayden-Gouvis, a very talented financial planner in her own right, offered candid advice on many aspects of the book and was a continual source of inspiration. It is very special to be helped by an exceptional daughter. I am also grateful for the good humor, love, and insight provided by Maura's husband Carlos Sadovi and their daughter Kyra, and Jamie's husband Jed Weissberg and their son Chet.

I am thankful for all the work that the *Game Plan*'s many ground troops—too numerous to mention—have done. For many months we've nudged and encouraged each other along. Now that we are finally airborne, we hope the fruits of our labor help you and your financial life to rise to the heights where you've always yearned to soar.

VERN C. HAYDEN

Contents

The Hayden Playbook

These 10 investing principles are integral components of the steps outlined in this book. Use these plays and you'll be well on your way to creating, working, and winning your investing game plan.

1. Protect that principal.

Hang on to the money you already have. That's the first rule of investing. Some loss some of the time is pretty inevitable in the stock market. But the best money managers limit injury to your portfolio and prevent unnecessary losses. In evaluating a mutual fund or even the performance of your overall portfolio, pay close attention to how the fund or portfolio fared in down years relative to its benchmark. It's more important that managers do better than the market on the downside than whether they outperform on the upside.

2. Be your own benchmark.

Benchmarks like the S&P 500 may hold the public spotlight, but they must be secondary to your personal benchmark. Focus on what returns you reasonably need to meet your goals. Knowing your benchmark can enable you to avoid assuming more risk than necessary. Keep your eye on your own game, not the one on the next field.

3. Buy and adapt.

A good investing game plan is not rigid. It's dynamic. Whether we're talking about your percentages in stocks versus bonds or your choice of specific mutual funds, you can't be afraid to change. Change can be good, if it's based on good reasons, such as the Great Bear Market of

2000–2002, a new and untested fund manager, or a sudden shift in your personal life. Structure and steadfastness are smart. Stubbornness is not. Just be sure your short-term actions don't unintentionally undercut your long-term game plan.

4. Whatever your age, get an offense and a defense.

Age gets too much focus in most financial planning assessments. Just because you're young doesn't mean you should be ultra-aggressive and lose all your money. You can never really make up time. In fact, youth is when you should be growing your money, not losing it. It is the early money you invest that compounds and grows the most dramatically over time. At the other extreme, there is no set age at which you can't afford some upside risk. Any age can warrant an investing offense and an investing defense.

5. Plan short term for the long term.

The financial planning profession loves a 30-year plan. But the prospect can be so daunting that it prompts people to give up any hope of planning at all. Avoid paralysis by breaking up your projections into time periods that are manageable for you. A solid five-year plan can be extremely effective. It guides and encourages you to act now—and now is the only time that you can invest money for your future.

6. Look at risk as well as returns.

Would you rather have a 50 percent chance at $10 or an 80 percent chance at $8? Although most people would pick an 80 percent chance at $8, that's not how they invest. They don't pay attention to the risk fund managers take to get the returns they post. Sometimes $8 is better than $10, if it means you're not jeopardizing your principal. Give risk its due, because the less you take, the better chance you have of not losing money or at least not losing as much.

7. Hit the books (or the Internet).

If you're a new investor, learn the differences between a stock, a bond, and a commodity. Once you have the basics down, there's always more to learn. Read good investment books, learn to distinguish between a sales pitch and sound advice, and then invest in what you know and whom you know. Whether you're a do-it-yourselfer or a client, homework pays off.

8. Avoid sectors unless you can handle the high-risk adrenaline rushes.

Industry sectors are sexy but dangerous, as they cycle in and out of favor so fast. Those tempted should keep their sector investments to small doses, pay close attention, and act quickly. If you want more excitement, I recommend Vegas.

9. Keep score.

The investment industry wants nothing more than for you to fork over your money and forget about it. But contrary to the blind buy-and-hold mantra, you should stay abreast of your investments. Knowing where your money is invested and how it's doing will help you make better decisions, not worse. Do-it-yourselfers should tally the progress of their investments twice a month (I check in on 421 funds every Friday). If you're working with an advisor you're not off the hook—you'll need to make sure he or she has a good system to track your progress and apprise you of developments. Just don't let the near-term focus make you lose track of your long-term strategy.

10. Be professional or get a professional.

If you measure up to the task of doing it yourself and you have the time, talent, and temperament to pull it off—that's great. If you don't, find a professional advisor who understands and can work with your resources, goals, and value system. Make sure your coach is giving you effective, honest, and objective plays to run with. It's your team and your game.

Introduction

Why You Need a Game Plan

It was Monday, April 11, six weeks into the Great Bear Market that first bared its teeth in the spring of 2000. The voice on the line sounded desperate. "Vern, my name is Jack, and I saw you on CNBC last Friday. What you said about planning makes a lot of sense. The problem is, I think it's too late for me. I'm an attorney. What I did was so stupid. My wife is ready to divorce me. I thought tech would go up and up, so I took $550,000—all of our savings—and borrowed another $150,000, and I plunked it all into tech stocks. Now I'm down to about $200,000. What should I do?" In the background, his wife sobbed, "I told him not to do it. But would he listen to me?"

Joe has a landscaping and contracting business. He and his wife Pam had most of their savings, about $70,000, in their 401(k). A couple in their early 30s, they were entranced with the power of the bull market. "We put it in the funds heavy in technology with the best five-year record. It seemed obvious that that was the wave of the future and tech was really on a roll. One of the funds was up 130 percent in 1999!" But like a block of ice carried down the street on a hot summer day, their investments melted away, by about 60 percent to only $28,000. To get back to even again, they have to make about 150 percent on what they've got left. As they are young, time may be on their side. But they'll need every minute of it.

Bill and his wife Judy, both corporate executives in their late 50s, had about $500,000 in investments at the beginning of 2000. He invested their money at the tail end of the boom in a portfolio that included numerous tech and aggressive growth funds and a smattering of seemingly solid stocks like General Electric. Then the bottom dropped out of the market. As his money dwindled, Bill expressed his concerns to his broker. The advice he got: Hang in there, a rebound's coming. It didn't. Instead, the couple rode the market down until they had lost half of what they had invested. By the time they arrived in my office on July 3, 2002, they felt defeated. It may be another five or 10 years before Bill and Judy fulfill their dream of retirement that had been just within their reach.

Maybe you're one of the fortunate ones that didn't lose money in the tech crash or the Great Bear Market that began in 2000 and was still raging through mid-2002. But the sad truth is most investors in the market did lose, far more than they should have in a typical market downturn. In the midst of the economic turmoil, September 11th happened. Between a tortuous volatile market and terrorist threats, many who once felt confident about investing are now, understandably, hesitant. I've taken panic calls from strangers around the country who have lost a lot of their money, in some cases all of it. Where did they go wrong?

- They had too much offense and not enough defense.
- They were not prepared for the mind-jarring swings stocks can take.
- They were more inclined to follow a hot sector trend than to stay on a diversified, seemingly stodgy track.
- They assumed that the almost unbearable pain of loss would soon enough lead to gain.
- They thought bad news would always be followed by good news.
- They thought the market would snap back quickly from any correction.
- They didn't adjust to market conditions by pulling back or even out of the market.
- They thought it was easy.
- They had no game plan.

These kinds of mistakes are only human. As investors, we can have a tendency to be overly confident and overly optimistic, especially during a prolonged bull market. But often these instincts work to our detriment. In recent years, they led many investors to big losses unrecoverable in the short run and perhaps not recoverable even in the long run. I am writing this book to help make sure these things don't happen to you. If they already did, I want to make sure they don't happen again.

My mission, my passion, and the purpose of this book are to help you achieve consistent returns on your investments while making sure you don't lose a bundle. Whether you're starting fresh or starting over, you need an investment game plan. This book will help you get one.

Just what is an investment game plan? It is an investment strategy designed to help an individual, couple, or family build wealth while avoiding painful and damaging financial losses. It's partly about picking the right investments. But it's also partly about having the *confidence* that you've put your investing house in order. Over time, those investments and that confidence work together to your benefit. If your game plan is producing solid returns you'll have confidence in it, even if it's not topping the charts. And if you have confidence in your game plan, you'll have the peace of mind to make wise investing decisions in times of panic or euphoria. Panics do happen, and not just in the market. Whether it's the sudden loss of a job, an unexpected death in the family, even a terrorist attack, a game plan can enable you to survive a personal financial crisis.

More than any single stock, single mutual fund, or single buy or single sell order that you may place, a game plan is the key to successful investing. A game plan is actually fairly easy to devise and maintain. Which is why it's ironic—and sad—that so few people have one. From what I have observed in my 35 years as a financial planner, the lack of a game plan is the common denominator of investors' woes.

After the grim markets of 2000 and 2001 and 2002, many investors sense the need for a game plan. But they don't know quite how to go about getting one. That's where I believe I can help.

As a Certified Financial Planner in private practice with more than three decades of experience, I've helped hundreds of real people meet their financial goals. I have tried a lot of different strategies. Some worked; some didn't. In the process, I have come to understand how to overcome the personal and market-related obstacles that typically prevent investors from turning financial dreams into realities. At the same time, as a long-time active member and former board member of the College for Financial Planning, I've also kept abreast of the big-picture changes that have shaped the financial services industry—and your portfolio.

Although I didn't live through the stock market crash of 1929, I have lived through numerous market cycles, and I'd like to share some of the lessons I've learned along the way. In the midst of the turmoil of 2002, when the Standard & Poor's 500 Index fell as much as 49.1 percent from its high in 2000, I was reminded of the bear market of 1973–1974 when I was selling mutual funds and real estate. At the time the stock market seemed like it was going to go down forever.

That's the sneaky thing about a down market. Eventually it makes you feel like you have as much of a chance of winning as a bug on a highway trying to face down 18-wheelers. Back in the early 1970s, I remember getting up every morning and watching the S&P 500 Index lose a few more points. Ultimately it amounted to a painful loss in its value of about 42 percent from the beginning of 1973 through 1974.

A lot of people learned the wrong lesson from this tough time. They sold their mutual funds and stocks and never did get back into the market. By playing it very safe, they may have protected their remaining money in the short term. But they also never made up their losses. This points out the importance of maintaining a flexible attitude toward investing. Just as I don't believe in blindly buying and holding, I also think it's a mistake to sell out and never buy back in.

It was during the early 1970s that I came to understand that there are the two major investing risks. There is the more obvious risk of losing actual money and the somewhat subtler risk of missing out on opportunities to increase your wealth through investing. If you've taken a more aggressive approach than you can stomach, you may react to losses in a volatile market by pulling completely out. But if you never take another investment risk, there's very little hope that you'll ever make the money back.

I saw this sad scenario play itself out back in 1975 when the econ-

> *Hayden Play:*
> **Buy and adapt.**
>
> A good investing game plan is not rigid. It's dynamic. Whether we're talk-ing about your percentages in stocks versus bonds or your choice of specific mutual funds, you can't be afraid to change. Change can be good, if it's based on good reasons, such as the Great Bear Market of 2000–2002, a new and untested fund manager, or a sudden shift in your personal life. Structure and steadfastness are smart. Stubbornness is not. Just be sure your short-term actions don't unintentionally undercut your long-term game plan.

omy improved and the market started to turn around. A lot of people, burned by their losses, weren't there to enjoy the gains. By the end of the year the S&P 500 was up about 31 percent. In 1976 it was up 19.2 per-cent. Within about three years the S&P 500 recovered. But the investors who dropped out of the market after the S&P 500's 29.8 percent drop in 1974 never experienced this rebound.

Fast-forward to the recent past. I don't need to tell you that the car-nage is even worse this time. From the beginning of 2000 through 2002, investors watched in disbelief as the value of some of their retirement funds and college tuition funds shrank by half or more and their financial lifeboats were tossed about. By the middle of 2002, CEOs of major com-panies were being hauled off in handcuffs and several brokerage houses were discredited.

The American public lost confidence in corporate America and the stock market. Suddenly the basic ideas, concepts, and strategies that had guided people on how to invest in the market were up for grabs. Funds that bet against our country's great companies were cleaning up. Many reaped returns of up to 70 percent or more in 2001 and 2002, largely by short selling—essentially by betting that shares would fall. The Prudent Bear fund was one of them, posting a whopping 57.6 percent return from January 2002 through early August of 2002.

So what do you do? How do you make sense of the financial world when confusion reigns? Do you put all your money into the most recently anointed "safe havens" of gold, real estate, natural resources, and emerging markets? Or do you stay with your current diversified buy-and-hold strategy? Is active or fixed allocation right for you?

Unfortunately, neither I nor any other financial expert can claim to offer a perfect formula to help every investor through the next storm. But what I do know is that this kind of turmoil is exactly why you need the very clearly designed investing game plan that this book will help you get. A good game plan takes into account your personal and financial situation but also is nimble enough to respond strategically to changing conditions—be they internal in your own life or external in the market.

Readers of this book are all ages, have a variety of occupations, and aspire to different dreams and goals. Some have little or no money, and some have millions. Regardless of your situation, everyone needs a well-thought-out investing game plan. Take this 10-step process one step at a time and you'll have a plan that will last a lifetime. Here are just a few of the questions the 10 steps will address:

- How do I get my emotions to work *for* me, not *against* me, when it comes to investing?
- How do I figure out how much risk I should take?
- How do I figure out my goals?
- How much of my portfolio should be in offense, and how much in defense?
- Should I use mutual funds or individual stocks and bonds?
- Should I use index funds or actively managed funds?
- How do I figure out which funds to use?
- Who are some of the best fund managers?
- What are the best fund families?
- How do I track my investments to make sure they're working for me?
- Do I have to buy and hold?

In addressing these questions, the key insights in this book aren't drawn solely from academic research. When I manage money, I'm not just focusing on numbers. Neither is any other Certified Financial Planner or advisor who is worth their salt. I see money and the people who own it as intrinsically connected. It's up to me to synthesize an individual's goals, risk tolerance, and his or her money into a workable investment game plan. As a Certified Financial Planner, I've been trained in holistic financial planning to do this, and I'll share this broad approach to addressing the variables of your situation as we begin planning your game plan together.

Though I will present the most compelling theories and studies on investing, my perspectives are ultimately real-world perspectives. They come from experience gained in the mud of the marketplace and from working with real people as clients. There are no untested hypotheses here, just tried-and-true experience.

Through my experience, I've framed a 10-step approach to getting an investing game plan, with the steps grouped in three parts:

Invest in Yourself

1. Get the "game plan mind-set"—commitment, consistency, courage.
2. Know your risk tolerance.
3. Know your goals.

Create a Game Plan

4. Get the fund fever.
5. Get an offense and a defense.
6. Pick the players.
7. Know your team.
8. Get to know the players.

Stay the Course

9. How ya doin'?
10. Write it up!

Finally, for those who suspect they can use some assistance in getting an investing game plan—and for reasons I'll describe later I think almost anyone can benefit from good, unbiased advice—the final chapter discusses how to seek out and size up financial advisors.

The Big Picture

This book, then, is about the 10 steps to a successful investing game plan. But investing is only part of your financial life. It may well be the most important part of your financial picture long-term. But it's only part. Here are seven other parts:

1. *Cash Flow Planning.* Where does your money for daily living come from, and how is it being spent?
2. *Tax Planning.* More than filing a tax return, this area includes issues like whether to invest in a traditional or Roth individual retirement account (IRA), how much tax you save in a 401(k) plan, and whether you should use a Section 529 educational savings plan.
3. *Retirement Planning.* Some people prefer to think of retirement planning in terms of financial freedom or independence from an employer or from worry. Whatever it means to you, living without a fresh stream of steady income takes advanced planning.
4. *Estate Planning.* You've poured your life's work into building an estate, and you need to do some planning to protect and distribute it. Estate planning is all about who you want to get what and when, and how you can avoid giving it all to Uncle Sam.
5. *Insurance.* Insurance covers all areas, including life, health, cars, other property, potential liabilities, and long-term health care. This is a big, complicated, and important subject.
6. *Special Issues.* This catchall category includes things like providing for education, elderly parents, disadvantaged kids, and gifted kids.
7. *Life Planning.* This is a subject that's financial not in its core but in its reverberations. It includes life changes like a career change or moving to a new location.

Take a moment to think about each of these areas in your own life. If there were a spectrum between where you are and where you want to be, what would it look like?

Picture a chart like Table I.1. The gap between the end of each arrow

Table I.1   **Financial Planning Spectrum**

Area		Target
Investments	⟶	X
Cash Flow	⟶	X
Tax	⟶ Gaps	X
Retirement	⟶ to	X
Estate	⟶ Be	X
Insurance	⟶ Closed	X
Special Issues	⟶	X
Life Planning	⟶	X

and the target represents issues that still need to be resolved in each area. Mapping each factor this way triggers a process of identifying your needs and beginning to address them. Though each issue is a separate line, they all belong on one chart. It's the interaction among these several parts that ultimately makes the whole financial planning process work. Just as in football, basketball, or soccer, each player has a position; it is the interaction of the team members that determines the team's success. This book focuses on one particular part of the picture—investing. But as I discuss the investment game plan, I'll make clear how it can impact the other areas of your financial life.

Throughout the past three years, my office has been inundated with people who called looking for advice after losing money. I asked each of them the following question: "Did you have any kind of written game plan?" *Not one did!* I want to make sure that doesn't happen to you. So let's get started on yours!

Chapter 1

Step 1: Get the
Game Plan Mind-Set
Commitment, Consistency, Courage

In late 2001 I received a call from a woman named Debbie. About five years earlier she had invested about $50,000, almost entirely in tech stocks. By March 2000 some of Debbie's picks were up 300 percent, and her original chunk was worth about $170,000. But as tech started to plunge that year, her portfolio did, too. In six weeks she lost over 40 percent. By the year's end she had only $42,000: five years, and an $8,000 loss from her original principal.

Why did this happen to Debbie? Why did this happen to thousands of people? Why did this happen to you? The tactical reason is that Debbie made a huge investment in a single sector without cushioning the tremendous risk she incurred. It's a critical misstep. But the more fundamental reason is that Debbie did not have a belief system guiding her strategies. If you are going to invest money, you need a belief system.

Most of my life I've played sports, and for the past 44 years handball's been my game. When I first started I thought it was an easy game: just hit a hard little rubber ball around a large rectangular court wearing the leather gloves. I did a lot of chasing, and a lot of losing. Determined to get better, for two years in a row I enrolled in a weeklong handball camp in Durango, Colorado, taught by Pete Tyson and John Bike. Pete, a former champion, has been handball coach at the University of Texas for 30 years. John was the current world handball champion. These guys were the masters. How did they start the camp? Not on the handball court, but off, teaching us their belief system for the game. Without those beliefs, they explained, even the fastest runner and sharpest hitter would be left flailing. Only after a grounding in the beliefs behind the game could a player expect to develop winning strategies and tactics on the court.

Tyson and Bike's belief system was focused on three C's—commitment, consistency, and courage. I've adopted them not only on the handball court, but for my financial planning clients and, in fact, in many areas of my life. The three C's are intangibles, but they're the key to getting tangible results.

Commitment

The first C is commitment. I'm not talking about a congenial get-acquainted handshake here. If you're going to invest you need a commitment to:

- Discipline.
- Confidence in the long-term viability of American industry.
- Continued learning.
- Yourself and your family.

A Commitment to Discipline

Most of us have a love/hate relationship with discipline. We hate to go through the rigors that discipline demands, but we are pleased with and proud of the outcome it produces. We hate dieting, but we like losing weight. We loathe going to the gym, but we like to be fit.

Discipline means doing what you rationally know is good for you when you feel like doing something else. It's tough in all areas of life, but it's especially tough in investing, where our psychological makeup often does not work in our financial favor. For example, we get the urge to sell when our investments are suffering, even though that's often the worst time to bail out. There may be a time to dump a stock, but you shouldn't automatically react to the normal ups and downs of the market. We buy when the market is upbeat, even though that's when we pay top dollar. In fact, individual investors' reactions to the market are so counterproductive that professionals measure them to find out what *not* to do. When a consumer sentiment index indicates investors are bullish, that's when pros want out. When the small fry are nervous, the pros want in.

There are many other examples of knee-jerk reactions determining our financial fate. For example, studies have shown that people feel more strongly about the pain of loss than the pleasure of equal gain. What does that mean in practice? As Gary Belsky and Thomas Gilovich point out in their book, *Why Smart People Make Big Money Mistakes—and How to Correct Them,* if you feel more strongly about avoiding loss than securing gain, you end up doing things like panic selling out of wise investments because they take a temporary dip. (Selling could be a smart move in a prolonged bear market. But all too often it's done in a panic, and not as part of a reasoned adjustment to your portfolio.) In a different manifestation of the same tendency, investors hold on to losing investments in hopes of avoiding having to lock in a loss.[1] What does it take to avoid these impulses? Tremendous discipline.

Even if what you've got in your portfolio is doing well, you might feel lousy if your neighbor's is doing better. Suddenly you may find yourself trading in what you've got for what he's got, just when what he's got is hot—namely, expensive. According to Dalbar, a Boston-based financial research firm, that tendency to chase performance—and arrive late to the game—manifested itself in spades in the 1990s. "Individuals who are generally free to act on their own tend to overreact," says Dalbar president Louis Harvey. "People tend more recently to pile on when the market is really high. They tend more to buy high than to sell low, which is quite a significant change over the last decade or so."

What's the upshot of this impulsive behavior? In most cases, worse returns. A Dalbar study of mutual fund flows from 1984 through 2000 showed that the average investor in stock mutual funds earned 5.3 percent a year, while the S&P 500 earned 16.3 percent a year. Some of that differential may be due to good reasons to sell, like using money to buy a home or finance a college education. But some of it is surely due to investors selling out of a desire to get out or avoid missing out.

There's an impulsive investor in all of us, and that's why discipline in its many manifestations is so important. There's the discipline to set aside a certain amount of your income each month for investments, the discipline to stick with your plan when part of your portfolio is struggling, the discipline to stick with your plan when other investments are putting up higher numbers, the discipline to stay diversified among a number of different investments, the discipline to monitor your investments.

I'll talk about the tactical reasons for many of these moves throughout the book. But behind them all is a basic belief that it takes discipline to succeed at investing. If you're not ready to be disciplined, then you're not ready to invest.

A Commitment to Confidence in the Long-Term Viability of American Industry

Investing in the U.S. stock market (and the bond market, for that matter) is a statement of confidence in the future of the American economy. Stock shares represent ownership in a company and therefore a stake in its profits. If companies earn money—and more of it—over time, stock prices eventually follow suit.

If we look back at history we have good reason to believe that U.S. companies will continue to grow. If you have any doubt, consider the U.S. gross domestic product, a measure of the country's output of goods and services. For most of our lifetimes, it has steadily risen—from $91.3 billion in 1930 to $10.1 trillion in 2001, according to the U.S. Department of Commerce's Bureau of Economic Analysis. In Table 1.1 you can see that it has had only seven annual declines.

It's a simple enough concept intellectually. But sometimes it's not so easy to believe. When the economy is in a recession, when your friends are getting laid off, when the Securities and Exchange Commission

Table 1.1   Gross Domestic Product: U.S. Gross Domestic Product Annual Growth 1930–2001—Annual Percentage Change from Preceding Year

Year	Change	Year	Change
1930	−12.0	1966	9.6
1931	−16.1	1967	5.7
1932	−23.2	1968	9.3
1933	−4.0	1969	8.1
1934	16.9	1970	5.5
1935	11.0	1971	8.6
1936	14.2	1972	9.9
1937	9.7	1973	11.7
1938	−6.3	1974	8.3
1939	6.9	1975	8.9
1940	10.1	1976	11.5
1941	25.0	1977	11.4
1942	27.7	1978	13.0
1943	22.7	1979	11.8
1944	10.7	1980	8.9
1945	1.5	1981	12.0
1946	−0.3	1982	4.1
1947	10.0	1983	8.5
1948	10.3	1984	11.3
1949	−0.7	1985	7.1
1950	10.0	1986	5.7
1951	15.4	1987	6.5
1952	5.6	1988	7.7
1953	5.9	1989	7.5
1954	0.3	1990	5.7
1955	9.0	1991	3.2
1956	5.5	1992	5.6
1957	5.4	1993	5.1
1958	1.4	1994	6.2
1959	8.4	1995	4.9
1960	3.9	1996	5.6
1961	3.5	1997	6.5
1962	7.5	1998	5.6
1963	5.5	1999	5.6
1964	7.4	2000	5.9
1965	8.4	2001	2.6

Source: U.S. Department of Commerce.

(SEC) seems daily to find yet another company that inflated its earnings through aggressive accounting, it can be hard to have confidence in the future of American business. If history, though, is our guide, we know that business is cyclical. Even after rough troughs, capitalism presses on. And as for bookkeeping, ultimately the scrutiny that accounting scandals engender helps make the public markets more credible, and in turn stronger.

Indeed, sometimes the problem is not that investors are skeptical of our nation's economic future, but that they are not skeptical enough. During the hypergrowth years of 1998 and 1999, the seductive siren song that blinded so many people to some basic investment truths went like this: "Technology is the world of the future, and it will continue to change our lives forever! We can't go wrong investing in technology—it's a whole new economy!" Of course, it's now clear that while technology will continue to affect our lives, not every tech stock has a future worth investing in. But if the engine of our industrial, technical, and informational culture keeps moving forward, and you believe that it will continue to do so, then you should commit to invest in American business.

A Commitment to Continued Learning

Investing is an endeavor that benefits from continued learning. Some people embrace the topic of investing and strive to master the challenges of analyzing company fundamentals, deciphering charts, and screening stocks. For others, investing is not that kind of passion. They want minimal intellectual involvement. But either way, investing takes a certain amount of understanding of the behavior of the markets and the traders and investors who operate in them daily. Investing is not like getting your driver's license—one test and you're done. You've got to gain a baseline understanding and build on it through reading, listening, and exchanging ideas with the many others who are trying to make sense of the market's unpredictability.

I have been in this business for 35 years. I still find myself constantly challenged, and challenging myself, with new studies, perspectives, and points of view on investing. My commitment to learning about investing has become a regular and stimulating part of my life. To the degree appropriate, it should be the same in yours.

A Commitment to Yourself and Your Family

I don't care whether you are rich or not so rich, whether you've got a big job or no job, whether you've made a lot of money mistakes or a lot of good money moves. Whatever your situation, you deserve to have the best money management available to you. What does available mean? Perhaps you are the best person to manage your family's money. Perhaps investing is an interest or passion, and you feel confident in your skills. But if it's not—if you're not certain that you're the top choice—then you owe it to yourself and your family to find that person. As a Certified Financial Planner, obviously I'm a big believer in the benefits of good advice—not *all* advice, but *good* advice. I explain various ways to get help, and the various costs of assistance, in Chapter 11. For now the key is to recognize that you and your family deserve a top-notch investing game plan. You need to make a commitment to yourself to deliver it.

Consistency

The second C is consistency. Consistency can have a lot of meanings. Fundamentally, being a successful investor demands that your behavior be consistent with your belief system. But the way I think most about consistency is as an approach to get results. Whatever your goal may be—and this is not limited to investing—there are usually two ways to achieve it: the slow and steady, incremental approach or the big-hit method. With the big-hit method, you essentially go for broke—putting all your chips into one play, one client, one starvation diet. If it works at all, it works big. But even then, the big-hit results usually are not long-lasting.

The consistent tactic can be much more tedious. Decades ago, when I used to sell financial products, we called it the water torture way. Some folks in the office would ignore the little clients and just hustle for a whopping sale. Others of us would take any client we could get, making any sale we could close and slowly build a clientele. *Drip, drip, drip.* Enough drips—enough commissions—you had yourself a living, a living that did not depend on any single client or single sale.

The same philosophy can apply to nearly any aspect of life. You don't lose weight by starving yourself one day and gorging the next. You don't get into shape by playing football with the guys Thanksgiving morning and then spending the next three days eating stuffing on the couch. You lose weight and get into shape by consistently eating fewer fattening foods and working out a certain number of days each week. The theory even applies to familial relationships. One family vacation a year cannot compare with the value of spending a consistent amount of time with your spouse and children each weekend or each day.

Consistent behavior is less dramatic, perhaps, but more productive than big hits. And that's especially true with investing. Why? Because the market is pretty darn efficient. If a stock or certain group of stocks becomes extremely highly valued—the big hit—it's usually got more to do with that pile-on effect Dalbar's Louis Harvey mentioned earlier than actual business fundamentals. When something seems like it's got big-hit potential, everybody piles on. At the first sign of trouble, they pile on out. Most investors are like my friend Debbie with her $50,000—they don't get out fast enough and are left with little to show for their efforts. That's why it's better to shoot for consistent results rather than big hits.

How can you apply a belief in consistency to your own investing game plan? Consistent behavior takes many forms. One example is what's called rebalancing. Say you make a decision that as part of your game plan you are going to invest 5 percent of your funds in a large-cap growth mutual fund. If six months later that 5 percent has grown to 15 percent, while your view of the fund category is essentially the same, then consistent behavior would mean you'd sell a portion of that position to bring your exposure back down toward 5 percent.

There are other ways of staying consistent: saving a certain amount of income each month, or automatically investing a portion of your earnings every quarter, or reviewing your portfolio thoroughly, twice a year. The key is to create a structure for your investing habits so that you don't find yourself reacting in the moment, to your detriment. Consistent behavior represents a recognition that, if left to their own devices, your emotion-driven actions might not get you the investing results you seek. By creating a systematic action plan based on your beliefs, you reduce the odds that impulsiveness, overconfidence, or those old market foes—fear and greed—will prompt you to cater to momentary emotion at the expense of long-term financial gain.

Courage

Consistency may sound sensible enough. But in the throes of market gyrations, sticking to a consistent course takes courage—courage to follow through on your belief, courage to stand by your commitment, courage to resist the trend and stay on track with your plan. Courage is an elusive quality for even the most sophisticated investor. Managers of large institutional accounts are notorious for behaving like sheep—purchasing stocks for no other reason than because others are doing the same. Probably the most glaring example of this phenomenon is the rapid rise, and fall, of technology stocks in the late 1990s.

As recently as the middle 1990s, tech stocks were a niche play pursued by the most aggressive investors. But as a few high-profile names enjoyed wild successes—the initial public offering (IPO) of Internet browser software maker Netscape Communications, the emergence of PC maker Dell Computer, the rapid growth of software maker Microsoft and chip shop Intel, and the dominance of networker Cisco Systems—suddenly even the sleepiest and shiest of investors could not get into technology, and Internet stocks in particular, fast enough.

Catering to demand, mutual fund companies that once offered just an aggressive growth or perhaps even a technology fund suddenly started to present a whole menu of tech choices—new technology funds, information technology funds, Internet funds, Internet B2B (business-to-business) funds, and "NexTech" funds. Indeed, the number of new tech mutual funds introduced went from 12 in 1998 to 42 in 1999 to 90 in 2000, according to fund data tracker Morningstar (see Table 1.2). And the funds performed, for a while. For the year 1999, more than 100 mu-

Table 1.2   Tech Fund Madness

Year	New Tech Mutual Funds
1994	4
1995	4
1996	9
1997	12
1998	12
1999	42
2000	90
2001	7

Source: Morningstar.

tual funds, mostly invested at least 50 percent in technology, returned *more than 100 percent.*

How did the tech craze happen? Of course books could—and have—been written on the subject. But the basic behavior was this: When people saw the prices of tech stocks rising so high so fast, they wanted a piece of the action. Individual and institutional investors alike bought in, thereby driving the prices of the stocks higher. Once the bubble began to burst in the spring of 2000, there was not enough in the way of fundamental value—earnings—in these companies to support their wild prices. As swiftly as the prices rose, they collapsed. The Nasdaq closed out 2000 down 39 percent, and 2001 down 21 percent. From the high of March 10, 2000, to the end of 2001 the Nasdaq lost more than 70 percent of its value.

In the most manic part of this period, it would have taken an incredible amount of courage to invest in anything *but* tech. Yet, unless you were one of the savviest—and strongest willed—investors, an investor who ducked out before the bottom fell out, you'd probably would have been better off in almost anything but tech.

To see why, let's compare two funds, First Eagle SoGen Global, an international stock and bond fund, and John Hancock Technology, a tech stock fund. In 1998, the Hancock tech fund returned 49.2 percent, an enviable return by almost any measure. An investor drawn to that impressive performance would have been rewarded in 1999 in spades, with an eye-popping 132.3 percent return. Meanwhile, SoGen lost 0.3 percent in 1998 and returned "only" about 19.6 percent in 1999. At that point a frustrated SoGen investor might have jumped ship. To what end? The Hancock fund lost over 37 percent in 2000 and another 43 percent in 2001. Meanwhile, SoGen returned about 10 percent both years— doing far better than both the tech-laden Nasdaq index and the broader S&P (see Table 1.3).

Over five years through September 30, 2002, SoGen's annual return of 7.29 percent is significantly better than Hancock Tech's 14.6 percent loss. Over 10 years through September 30, 2002, the compound annual returns were: 10.3 percent for SoGen versus 4.3 percent for Hancock. But through the decade SoGen's returns were much steadier with substantially lower risk. There were no panics with SoGen. One wonders how many Hancock investors got into the fund just in time for the abominable results.

The Hancock tale is not unusual. Take a look at the returns of several onetime outstanding performers in Table 1.4.

Courage to stay your own course demands the ability both to pass on the current trends and to stand by the principles of your investing game plan. Of course, it's tough to be courageous if your portfolio is in the tank. If your investments are sinking while your office mate is making a big hit in, say, biotech, you may feel more like a sucker than courageous.

Table 1.3 **Steady Eddie versus Hot Hand: Annual Returns of SoGen Global versus John Hancock Technology***

	1998	1999	2000	2001
SoGen Global	−0.3%	19.6%	9.7%	10.2%
John Hancock Technology	49.2%	132.3%	−37.2%	−43.1%

Source: Morningstar.
*It should be noted that these funds invest in different assets and serve different purposes. In addition, remember that past performance should not be considered indicative of future results.

Table 1.4 Onetime Outstanding Performers: Annual Returns

	1998	1999	2000	2001
Alliance Tech Class A	63%	72%	–25%	–26%
PBHG Tech & Comm.	26	244	–44	–52
Pimco Innovation	79	139	–29	–45
Munder Net Net	98	176	–54	–48
Firsthand Tech Value	24	190	–10	–44
VanWagoner Tech	85	224	–28	–62

Source: Morningstar.

That's why it's important to choose a selection of investments that's likely to produce steady positive returns in any market environment.

If you have a portfolio with investments that, while not necessarily hitting the top of the charts, are on the whole consistently doing well, you'll be less tempted by the latest, greatest thing. Say, for example, one of your investments, a value fund, is not performing as well as growth stocks with high earnings expectations. You're tempted to sell your value fund to buy some growth. If you've already got some growth in your portfolio, that growth fund will likely satisfy your itch and reduce the chances you'll sell out of the value fund at its low, just before it may rebound.

By having some growth and some value—by diversifying your investments—you are likely to earn returns that are more steady than spectacular. A burst in one area will be undermined by a lag in another. But it's an approach that could make you more likely to *behave* in a way that will *preserve* those steady returns than if you were constantly trying to bail out of trailing investments and hop onto hot ones. That's what diversification and allocation, which I discuss in Chapter 4, are all about. It's easier to turn your back to the trend when what you've got is doing just fine, thank you. If a game plan is at least doing what you expected it to do, then you'll be better able to resist the temptation to sell out at a low or buy the trend at its high. A game plan worthy of your confidence should give you the courage to stand by it.

The hardest thing to know, of course, is whether an investment is just in a temporary rut or it really was a subpar choice and you need to sell. I don't recommend blind buy and hold. In Chapter 9, I discuss reasons why at times you should cut the cord. That takes courage, too. But often the courage you need to muster is the courage to do nothing at all.

The Three C's, the Market, and Your Brain: A Challenging Trio

If you still don't think commitment, consistency, and courage are important to your investing game plan, consider what they're up against. Recent developments in neuroscience have underscored just how biologically primed our human brains are to want the fast buck—and to overlook the risk of losing even more.

Journalist Jason Zweig recently wrote in *Money* magazine about scientists' growing understanding of how investors' brains work.[2] By learning about the preprogrammed mechanisms that can fuel common investing mistakes, he argued, we take one step closer to circumventing them. I agree. So what should you know about your brain? Here are some of the recent findings that Zweig explored:

- *Fight or Flight.* For starters, the amygdala in the forward lower area of the brain responds with lightning speed to perceived threats. This was helpful when we were hunter-gatherers running from predators. But, as investors, the panic that ensues can derail a long-term investing strategy. That said, the memory of the fear and anxiety created by the amygdala may also be helpful, as it makes investors more cautious. Experiments by neurologist Antoine Bechara of the University of Iowa have indicated that people with damaged amygdalas never learn to avoid making riskier choices. It makes sense, then, Zweig pointed out, that investors accustomed to only the bull markets of the 1990s (and no past memories of fear to measure danger against) made too many risky choices.
- *Primed to Predict.* Thanks to two areas of the brain, the nucleus accumbens (at the bottom surface of the front of your brain) and the anterior cingulate (in the central frontal area), humans can't help themselves when it comes to patterns. It seems we're always looking for them in the

(Continued)

The Three C's, the Market, and Your Brain:
A Challenging Trio (Continued)

world around us. We respond unconsciously, Zweig says. Scott Huettel, a neuroscientist at Duke University, found that our brains expect a repetition after a stimulus occurs only twice. Fear and anxiety often occur when a repeat pattern is broken. This may explain why investors jump out of previously predictable companies when they miss earnings forecasts, Zweig says.

- *The Dopamine Buzz.* Dopamine is the brain chemical that gives you that euphoric feeling when you win big. It may come as no surprise that a team of scientists led by Harvard's Hans Brieter found a similarity between the brains of people trying to predict a future financial gain and the brains of cocaine addicts. Eventually investors get higher from the rush of dopamine they get when predicting a win than from the win itself, Zweig says. If the gain doesn't arrive, that euphoria quickly turns into depression.

How to harness all this knowledge? Zweig rightly points out that the science makes clear how important good, irreversible investing habits are to neutralizing the brain's propensities. Getting a disciplined game plan mind-set, then, is crucial to winning—and triumphing over biology.

Step 1, Get the Game Plan Mind-Set: Summing Up

Step 1, then, is not about calculating long-term financial needs or analyzing mutual fund returns. It's about getting the game plan mind-set. You can't turn it on like a switch. But you've got to start somewhere. Begin to think about the three C's, and keep them in mind throughout this book. Eventually they will form a belief framework that will serve you well throughout your investing life.

Chapter 2

Step 2: Know Your Risk Tolerance

At 3,000 feet, hands on the wing strut, wind in my face, I pushed into space. Spread-eagled, I shut my eyes and prayed! Thankfully, the static line automatically opened my chute. I was alive and euphorically floating to a successful landing. It was 1962 at a New York parachuting center. We were four guys on a dare. After an hour of training, two of us had the courage to jump. The other two became lifelong chickens.

Three months later, I heard that a fatal accident occurred at the parachute center and it was forced to close due to alleged safety violations.

Be that as it may, I never jumped again. I learned a lot about risk from that experience. The risk in jumping is losing your life. But the first-order risk—in life and in investing—is in not understanding risk.

If, after reading the preceding chapter, you believe you are ready to make a commitment to investing, and if you believe you have the courage to stand by that commitment, then you need to be prepared to take some risk. What exactly does that mean?

Let me be as clear and direct as possible.

There are two basic financial risks to investing: the risk of losing your money and the risk of losing an opportunity to make money. The two risks are in conflict. If you try to make money through certain investments, you could lose some or all of the money you invest. If you keep your money completely safe, you may miss out on the chance to earn good returns through investing.

The challenge of investing is to try to give yourself the chance to make money while minimizing the risk of loss by building in downside protection. That's what a good defense is all about.

Beyond the risk of lost money and the risk of lost opportunity, there is a third risk you must consider: the psychological risk that you can't handle the amount of risk you've taken. I call this your risk tolerance. A game plan must strike the right balance for you between the two financial risks given your personal risk tolerance.

As I'll explain, how to balance the two financial risks depends largely on your goals, the subject of Chapter 3. Step 2, this chapter, is figuring out your risk tolerance. As with Step 1, part of this analysis depends on your beliefs.

The Guesswork of Risk

I advise people about risk nearly every day. But even for professionals like me, there is a lot of guesswork with risk. Since risk is all about what will happen in the future, the outcome is uncertain. They say you can't get reward without risk, but just because you take risk doesn't mean you'll get rewarded for it.

Even though I spent seven years as an Air Force officer, I can't personally measure or prevent all the risks in flying. I have faith in the numbers that seem to say it's safer than driving, and I trust a pilot and crew. But I still say a little prayer going down the runway—and did so even before 9/11.

What gave you the courage to do something that scared you? It probably had something to do with faith and trust. Theologians define faith as the substance of things hoped for and the evidence of things not seen. Trust is when you believe that somebody, including yourself, can and will do the right thing. You have faith in a result and trust in somebody to make it happen. This chapter is about helping you figure out how much risk you can handle so that when you create a game plan you'll be able to trust yourself to stick with it, and you'll have faith that it will be worth the risk.

Gap Analysis

Your investment portfolio carries risk. You have a certain risk tolerance. The question is: Does your investment portfolio's risk match your risk tolerance?

Too often the answer is no. Rather, there's a gap between the two, as financial planning researcher ProQuest describes it. My goal as a planner is to help you close the gap, that is, to help you align the risk profile of your portfolio with your risk tolerance.

To close the gap, you first need to identify how large it is. That task involves knowing both the risk profile of your portfolio and your own risk tolerance. In later chapters we discuss the risks of various investment portfolios. This chapter is about sizing up your personal risk tolerance.

This chapter includes a quiz that I believe can help you evaluate your tolerance for risk. But it's not the only quiz out there. In fact, ProQuest, based in Australia, has come up with an excellent 25-question risk-profiling questionnaire for individuals.

The ProQuest web site, www.proquest.com.au, is accessible by subscription, and the cost is a hefty one—designed to be borne by professionals, who can then give their clients the questionnaire. If you are working with a financial planner, ask whether he or she has heard of ProQuest. If the planner is a ProQuest subscriber, take the test, and discuss it with your advisor. You'll both learn something, and you'll get closer to closing that gap.

The No-Risk Stash

Before talking about what you *can* risk, we have to talk about what you *can't* risk. None of us ever wants to lose money, anytime. But certain money we simply cannot afford to lose. If we were to lose it, we could lose our home, we could lose our car, we could be forced to scale back on the basic day-to-day expenses that support our lives and our families.

You may recall earlier that I talked about financial planning as holistic, about how you can't entirely separate issues like cash-flow planning and mortgage responsibilities from your investment decisions. Risk planning is one of the times when that overlap comes into play.

Before thinking of how much risk you should take in the stock and bond markets, you need to decide what portion of your funds doesn't belong there at all. This determination may depend on factors such as your job stability, your daily financial commitments, your near-term plans for major purchases like a home, or your emotional needs for financial security.

The basic rule of thumb is that you should not put at risk money that you may need in the next five years. That's because historically a broadly diversified portfolio of U.S. stocks and bonds has produced positive returns over the vast majority of five-year periods, according to data tracker Ibbotson Associates, Inc. If you can wait five years to cash out of a broadly diversified portfolio, odds are very good that you'll come out ahead. If you can't wait that long, you may end up having to sell when prices are at an ugly low. (That goes for bonds, too; their value doesn't always go up.) If you have to sell after a short time period, you might not come up with the amount of money you need.

So before you think about the extent of risk you can take, you have to set aside the funds you can't risk at all.

Reasonable versus Extreme Risk

Once you have a sense of the funds you can spare for investing, you'll need to decide just how much risk to take with those funds. Unfortunately, all too often people skip this step. They think of investing money like gambling money. Once they decide how much they're willing to play with, they're willing to risk it all.

The second-largest tourist attraction in the world is Las Vegas. (The first, by the way, is Mecca.) And that's no coincidence. Vegas is all about short-term thinking—the most natural way to think when it comes to money. In Vegas people roll the dice, spin a wheel, pull a handle, or play a hand, and voilà—instant gratification—win or lose!

The builders of the Vegas casinos knew how to stack the deck in their favor. Sure, there's some skill involved, sometimes. But most of the time if you win it is because you are lucky. Most of the time people take huge risks and sustain huge losses.

Hayden Play:
Look at risk as well as returns.

Would you rather have 50 percent chance at 10$ or an 80 percent chance at $8? Although most people would pick an 80 percent chance at $8, that's not how they invest. They don't pay attention to the risk fund managers take to get the returns they post. Sometimes $8 is better than $10, if it means you're not jeopardizing your principal. Give risk its due, because the less you take, the better chance you have of not losing or at least not losing as much.

If you want the instant gratification that comes with gambling, do it in Vegas. The only way to get immediate gratification in the markets is through extreme risk, like betting a bundle on one small up-and-coming stock or one white-hot sector. Extreme risk is like roulette: It offers a chance at a super-high return if you bet right, but there is also an extremely high chance of total wipeout.

The stock market is not a place to fool around with extreme risk. If you as an individual are going to invest your and your family's money in the market, you should subject it to only reasonable risk. Reasonable risk is the degree of risk you need to take to give yourself the chance to reach your goals, and not an iota more. If you estimate it takes an 8 percent annual return for the next five years to reach a short-term goal (and I'll talk about how to figure out the right percentage for you in the next chapter) then your game plan should be comprised of investments that together offer the best chance of providing you with that 8 percent return. Any combination of choices that proves even one bit more risky than that, and you are needlessly subjecting yourself to the possibility of losing your money.

Think of it like taking a trip. Say you have four days to drive 1,000 miles to your destination. If you drive 60 to 65 mph, you'll reach your destination in the time allotted. You'll incur the risk of getting behind a wheel and the risk of driving 65. But because driving about 65 mph is

> ### *I Can't Resist Extreme Risk!*
>
> If you know yourself well enough to recognize that at times you can't resist the market thrill of extreme risk, then you need to tweak your game plan to accommodate that yen in the least damaging way possible. Set aside a very small portion of your overall portfolio, no more than 5 percent, as a trading kitty. Go crazy chasing every hot stock tip you ever heard of. Just keep that kitty as far away as possible from the rest of your game plan.

necessary to your goal, and because a four-day trip is a reasonable goal, the four-day plan poses reasonable risk.

Say instead you're eager to drive 80 to 90 mph. You'd arrive a lot quicker and perhaps would have a less tedious trip. But you'd boost your chances of getting a speeding ticket or having a serious accident. The higher-speed driving subjects you to risks that you simply do not need to accomplish your goal. Likewise, euphoric tech returns of 98 or 99 percent may be thrilling, but a subsequent crash is not.

Risk Tolerance: The Risk That You Can't Handle the Risk

If you're still with me, then you're thinking that in the next chapter you're going to figure out your goals, figure out how much risk it'll take to try to achieve those goals, and then go for it. You'll venture forth into that five-year time horizon with the conviction that you'll have the courage to keep your commitment.

You'll go ahead and invest.

Now, what if three months later the market tanks? And tanks deeper? And now violence erupts overseas, and stocks drop again. A little rally perks up, but then oil prices spike, and it's six months later and you're down even more. Then the memorable words of Alan Greenspan, the head of the U.S. Federal Reserve, ring loud and clear. By mid-2002 he had declared that the country had shifted from a mood of "irrational exuberance" to one of "infectious greed." Corporate capitalism's integrity appeared to have broken down and the markets fell further.

At a time like this, the risk of losing money has materialized—you have far less than what you started with. Money that took you months or years to earn has evaporated. It's gone.

The optimist in you is trying to keep focused on that other risk of missed opportunity, the risk of not reaching your goals in 20 years if you're not in the stock market today. But as your mutual fund statements turn a deep red, you're tempted to bail out.

This temptation to sell or, on the flip side, to divert from your plan to chase a hot trend, is another risk of investing. It's separate from the risk of losing money or the risk of losing the opportunity to make money. It's psychological risk: the risk that you don't stick with your plan. When you look in the rearview mirror and see charts showing stock market behavior over the long term, it is easy to say "time cures risk." But what a long upward line doesn't show is the tremendous impact that a prolonged bear market can have on your emotions.

Even a two-year drop doesn't look so bad—unless you lived in it. Some of you may remember 1973–1974. It was like going down a flight of stairs. Some days the market was flat, and some days it was up a bit, but many more days it was down. After almost two years of this seasick journey, a lot of investors loss faith and trust in stocks. They deserted the market. The S&P 500 was down 37 percent. To make matters worse, inflation was up 22 percent over those two years. That is a 59 percent loss in purchasing power. The price of almost everything, especially gasoline (remember the lines?), was going up while individuals' wealth was plummeting. Few people maintained a consistent commitment to their investing plan back then because their courage understandably buckled.

Even within single years there's a lot of hidden trauma. The market dropped about 22 percent in one day on October 19, 1987. As many investors panicked out of the market, that October day changed a lot of living standards and a lot of careers on Wall Street. There was a tremendous run-up in the market prior to October 19. Many investors who had no disciplined game plan—or no tolerance to stand by their game plan—started running with the pack of lemmings toward the precipitous cliff. Some of those people who then sold out lost 20 to 25 percent of their money because they acted on this greed-fear double punch.

How about September 17, 2001, the first day the New York Stock Exchange opened following the terrorist attacks of September 11? The Dow Jones Industrial Average fell more than 7 percent that day, while the S&P 500 lost nearly 5 percent. Those kinds of nosedives are not easy for the most composed investor to withstand.

The long-term figures have a way of smoothing out those painful wrinkles. From 1926 through 2001, large-company stocks returned about 10.8 percent a year on average, according to Ibbotson Associates. So, time historically has ironed out the wrinkles. But you have to stay the course and get through those shorter-term traumas.

And it's not just traumas on the downside. It's also that pile-on effect mentioned in the prior chapter—people moving their money from stodgy investments to exciting ones, just in time for those hot items to fall from grace. I remember taking a phone call from a physician client in October 1999. His question was similar to the one I was hearing from many other clients: "Vern, do you think we should be in the Amerindo Technology fund? I hear it's really moving up and that the manager really knows his stuff when it comes to tech." Maybe he did, but at that time the fund was up about 146 percent. By the end of the year it was up 251 percent. Fearful of chasing hot money, I talked him out of the investment. I was sure he was upset with me for it. But in 2000 the fund lost 65 percent, and in 2001, 51 percent. What that meant was $10,000 grew to $35,100 and ended up being worth $6,019.

In the midst of the euphoria, the physician did not think he could bear the risk of missing out. But because he resisted the temptation, he managed to avoid losing money.

How can you manage to do the same? While part of the risk calculus you need to make is based on the goals you need to reach, part must be based on how much risk you can take psychologically—your risk tolerance.

What's Your Risk Tolerance?

One of my main tasks as a financial planner is to help people figure out not only their goals and the reasonable risks they need to incur to reach

The Scourge of Inflation

One risk that does not get the attention it unfortunately deserves is inflation. Inflation risk simply means that a dollar isn't worth what it used to be. What does inflation have to do with investing? A lot. If you want real growth in terms of buying power, then your investments have to outperform inflation. Inflation is insidious, sneaky, and in the long term a possible killer to your financial planning.

The difference between the inflation rate and your investment return is called "real return." It's kind of like in football, where no matter how many yards you gain, if you can't score a touchdown or a field goal you won't have any real victory.

Hopefully, everybody reading this book will live to age 67 and beyond. If you had lived the past 67 years, here is how inflation has affected you (years 1934–2001):

- First class postage went from 3 cents to 34 cents, an increase of 1,033 percent.
- The average automobile went from a cost of $1,436 to $17,120, an increase of 1,092 percent.
- A day in the hospital went from $12 to $2,808, an incredible gain of 23,300 percent.

Source: American Funds Distributors, Inc.

Recently, the inflation rate has not been too high, only 3.4 percent for 2000 and 1.6 percent in 2001, according to the U.S. Department of Labor's Bureau of Labor Statistics. But historically it has been much more painful. Table 2.1 shows the lifetime annual inflation rate for various periods. If you

Table 2.1   **Inflation for the Generations**

Year of Birth to 2002	Lifetime Average Annual Inflation Rate
1937–(65 years)	4.0%
1951–(50 years)	3.9
1961–(40 years)	4.4
1971–(30 years)	4.9
1981–(20 years)	3.5
1991–(10 years)	2.6

Source: Stocks, Bonds, Bills and Inflation® 2002 Yearbook, © 2002 Ibbotson Associates, Inc. Based on copyrighted works by Ibbotson and Sinquefield. All rights reserved. Used with permission.

The Scourge of Inflation (Continued)

presume an inflation rate of 3 percent going forward, you need to make sure that your game plan accounts for that rise. Stocks are a great defense against inflation because their earnings reflect the prices of goods and services. But bonds, so-called "fixed incomes," don't reflect price fluctuations. To the extent your portfolio is in fixed income investments or cash, you need to consider the risk of inflation as you plan to meet your goals.

those goals, but also their risk tolerance: the risk that they can't take risk. All the formulas in the world are useless if you're filled with dread each day over what's happening—or not happening—with your money. That's why this inquiry is critical before delving into the numerics of the game plan. Think of it as the calisthenics an athlete does before the actual game begins.

To help you figure out your risk tolerance, I've presented a list of questions very similar to the ones I pose to my clients. I use these questions to help clients design an investment strategy that they can stick with. If they're risk-averse investors, I don't want them to get too uncomfortable on the downside. If they're risk takers, I don't want them to get too antsy about missing upside. Why the customized tweaking? Because if either extreme happens, the investor will bolt from the plan. And that's where trouble happens.

As you take this quiz, don't try to pick the "right" answer. Try to be honest with yourself based on how you've acted in the past, or how you think you'd act in the future if you've already had some experience. That's the only way you'll be able to create a game plan that will work for you.

Before you begin, think broadly for a bit about how you would describe your ability to handle investment risk. Try to draw up, mentally or on paper, a descriptive statement. For example, "I can't handle losing money. The ups and downs of the market really bother me." Or "I know I have to take some risk, but I would consider myself a pretty conservative investor." Or "I get the idea of long-term investing and can't even be bothered paying attention day to day."

Risk Quiz

As you answer the quiz questions, write down your responses. Each time you choose a letter, give yourself one point for choosing an A, two points for a B, and three points for a C.

1. Your portfolio is invested partly in low-risk bond funds (about 40 percent) and partly in broadly diversified stock funds (about 60 percent), according to a long-term game plan. It's late spring, and this year your stock funds are not doing well. They're down about 5 percent, pretty much in line with the overall market. Wall Street analysts are divided on the market's future. You . . .

   A. Sell all of your stock funds and move the money to bond funds or cash.
   B. Stick with your allocation despite your current jitters.
   C. Would never be in bonds in the first place!

2. In the mid 1990s the S&P 500 funds posted double-digit returns—37 percent in 1995, 23 percent in 1996. Looked good to you, so you invested, too. Here are the returns on that investment for the next five years:

1997	1998	1999	2000	2001
33.2%	28.6%	21.1%	–9.1%	–12.0%

   During this period you . . .

   A. Can't take the pain of 2000 into 2001 and sell.
   B. Decide to hold through all five years.
   C. Bolt in 1999 for a tech fund posting triple-digit returns.

3. Your core fund with most of your investment money has returned about 9 percent a year over the past five years. But you read about

a health-care fund that's returned more than twice that for each of the past two years, and you're impressed with what you've read about the manager. You . . .

A. Do nothing.
B. Sell 5 percent of your core fund and invest the proceeds in the health-care fund.
C. Sell 35 percent or more of your core fund and invest the proceeds in the health-care fund.

4. Building on question 3, say you invested 5 percent of your portfolio in the hot-hand health-care fund, and after two great years this one fund now represents 12 percent of your portfolio. You . . .

A. Were the one who didn't invest in this fund back in question 3, and you still don't want any part of it.
B. Sell about half of the investment because, while you still have confidence, you want to take some money off the table.
C. Are so thrilled with this fund you add another 5 percent of your portfolio to it.

5. In early 2000, you learned of a tech fund that had been up 185.3 percent in 1998 and 232 percent in 1999. You invest. By the end of 2000 the fund has lost 76.3 percent, and few expect tech to rebound anytime soon. You . . .

A. Would never have touched this fund in the first place.
B. Sell and take the almost 25 percent of your investment you've got left.
C. Stay the course while you watch another 70 percent of what's left disappear in 2001.

How did you score? Everyone falls somewhere on the risk spectrum, as seen in Table 2.2. If you have only 5 to 7 points, then you're likely the type of investor who feels more comfortable giving up potential gains on the upside to cover your backside. You're risk averse. If you tallied 13 to 15 points, then you're an opportunistic investor who won't be satisfied

Table 2.2   The Risk Spectrum

	Risk Scale	
5–7 Points ———————	8–12 Points ———————	13–15 Points
Conservative	Moderate	Aggressive
(Risk averse)	(Risk steady)	(Risk seeker)

unless you're getting some piece of the moment's action. You're a risk seeker. If you have 8 to 12 points, you're the in-between type who'll be pretty content with a steady course. You're risk steady.

Should everyone aim to become a B? While it never hurts to try to temper emotional extremes, at a certain point that effort is counterproductive. If I've got a client who's queasy regarding the market and wants out, like person A in question 1, I may offer some reasons why I believe the investor ought to stay in. But if those reasons are not persuasive, ultimately I won't argue a person out of a decision. That's like trying to tell someone to forget about a headache: "Just don't let it bother you!" Well, if it is bothering you, then you're the one who has to live with that pain. You're the one who has to decide if it's worth it.

Step 2, Know Your Risk Tolerance: Summing Up

The second step in creating a game plan is figuring out your risk tolerance. Are you risk averse? Risk steady? Or a risk seeker? These aren't rigid categories, but by now you should have a feel for where you generally fit. You want to make sure there's no gap between the risk you're taking in your portfolio and your personal risk tolerance.

What will you do with this information? In Step 3, the next chapter, I'll help you figure out your investment goals. That's a mostly numerical exercise based on what you can save, how much time you've got ahead of you, and what lump sum you're shooting for. But now that you know your risk tolerance, you can put those Step 3 figures into context. If the numbers say you should take X amount of risk, but you know you're the risk-averse type, then you should ratchet down a notch or two. If the numbers produce a kind of steady Eddie portfolio that won't quench your thirst for some upside vim, you've got to build a little more risk into the picture in a way that will meet that need without threatening your overall plan.

We're not talking major surgery here. Just some tweaking around the edges to make sure you've got the right plan for you.

Chapter 3

Step 3: Know Your Goals

Successful marathoners start training months ahead. Whether it's a short three-miler or an arduous 19-mile trek, they know that a weekly regimen over many months is the key to performance on one day that seems far away. The only way to build up the stamina needed to finish the race, they say, is to follow your weekly mileage schedule as though it were a religion.

Financial goals require a similar approach. Just as running 26 miles six months from now can seem daunting, a 30-year financial plan with some pot-of-gold goal may seem outright impossible. The way to set and achieve financial goals is to focus less on a distant and intimidating figure than on what you can do this year, this month, or this day, to help yourself reach that target figure.

As a financial planner for the past 35 years, I've assisted many people in defining what they hope to accomplish financially. New clients inevitably feel they're in a chicken-and-egg situation. They are holding down jobs, forging ahead in careers, and saving some money. But they don't quite know how to go about investing because they don't know what they will need in the future. Not knowing where they need to be—lacking a target—sometimes they don't bother to invest at all.

Financial independence is the single most common objective my clients seek. But how does one quantify that? The term means something different for everyone. For one person it might mean moving to Mexico to live off Social Security checks. Others aim to build up two or three million dollars so they can remain in their own home but volunteer full time for their favorite charity. Still others want to be able to put all their grandchildren through college. There is one common denominator that many long-term dreams share: It takes a good chunk of time to save and invest enough money in order to live without working, or at least without worrying.

But how much time? And how much to save? And how to invest it? In an ideal world, 20-year-olds would sit down to figure out how much money they would need by the time they are 65 and then take precisely the steps necessary to reach that figure. They would know exactly how much they wanted to store up by the time they wanted to retire and how much they needed to invest in the short term to make it all happen. Then they would make it happen.

As you and I know, life is a lot messier than that. If you're young and starting a career and/or family or are in the early stages of either or both, you probably have trouble finding the time for a movie, let alone a moment to plan out the rest of your financial life. Plus, you face many variables and uncertainties that make planning seem senseless. Or perhaps you're in your 40s or 50s and have a better sense for your future. But you may feel too constrained by your current fiscal responsibilities (the mortgage, children's educations) to consider preparing for your own seemingly far-off future. Whatever your situation, none of us can afford to put off goal setting. And the task is not nearly so daunting as it seems. All good investing goals contain four key elements: (1) a certain time period over which you will invest and over which you'll assume (2) a specified annual rate of return, with an eye toward reaching (3) a lump-sum goal by saving (4) a specified amount on a regular basis.

This chapter discusses all four elements of goal-setting in sequence. Then I'll help you calculate your goals by breaking down the process.

Element One: A Manageable Time Period

The first element of a goal is choosing the proper time horizon. Just how many years out are you looking? As mentioned earlier in the Hayden

Playbook, there's nothing my industry likes more than a good 30-year plan. That's in part because long-term plans can smooth out the wrinkles of the markets while allowing the wonder of compounding interest to boost projections. It's also because ideally it would be nice if everyone sat down and figured out where they reasonably hoped to end up financially and then took steps every year to get there.

The multidecade concept, however, can be paralyzing. It's too hard for many to form a vision of where they want to be 30 years in the future. Intimidated, they don't plan—or invest—at all. To overcome this inertia, I suggest setting more manageable time-related goals. This means crafting short-term goals within 30-year plans where possible, or, if 30-year plans are just too tough, simply relying on short-term goals.

How short is short-term? About five years. Anything less than five years, and a goal might be more appropriately considered a budgeting exercise because it is less proactive about investing and more about how much you can save. Still, many times savings goals are the initial steps that you'll need to take to set yourself up to establish investing goals. Either way, as long as the targets are precise and realistic, they're keepers. And in all cases, my clients and I return to the here and now to set concrete challenges comprised of monthly and annual investing benchmarks. This is crucial because the present is the only time you can actually save and invest.

Hayden Play:
Plan short term for the long term.

The financial planning profession loves a 30-year plan. But the prospect can be so daunting that it prompts people to give up any hope of planning at all. Avoid paralysis by breaking up your projections into time periods that are manageable for you. A solid five-year plan can be extremely effective. It guides and encourages you to act now—and now is the only time that you can invest money for the future.

When to Start Planning

Now is when you should start to set goals. But so often people put off planning until their lives are more "settled." When is life ever really settled? If you want to wait until things settle down before you plan, you'll never plan. The conundrum brings to mind a young doctor who arrived at my office many years ago. The doctor, now one of this country's leading melanoma cancer experts, was starting his own private practice.

The 37-year-old was certain that he wanted to be financially independent in 30 years. And he was pretty certain he wanted to be living somewhere on the Monterey Peninsula, south of San Francisco. That was all we knew for sure. He didn't know what kind of salary he could hope to draw, how high his overhead would be, or who his patients would be. He didn't know how much money he would need to be financially independent.

So, in about the time it takes to plan a two-week river rafting trip, we started putting together a story about what his future financial life might look like. This was in 1972. We made all kinds of assumptions and guesses about this future: how much money he would make, how much his expenses would be, and how much money would be left over to invest.

We decided we could realistically shoot for a goal of an 8 percent annual return on investments because, based on historical data, it seemed like a reasonable return for a combination of all kinds of investments, including real estate. (Of course, any such return is not guaranteed. More about realistic returns later in this chapter.) Since we didn't know how much money he would actually be earning in salary, we left the amount to be invested to be determined annually. Over the years his earnings rose and we tweaked the annual investment amount upward. With tax-law changes and market shifts, we made adjustments in our investing targets along the way.

We couldn't plan out every day for 30 years, and we didn't try to. Instead, we moved the goal post in manageable chunks of time, looking out five years and tweaking annually. Eventually, our fictional tale became reality. The doctor now has two homes. One is in San Francisco, where he has cut back on the hours he spends at his practice. He plans soon to retire to his vacation home in Monterey, where he will keep his hand in the field of medicine that he so enjoys by taking a part-time consulting and teaching post.

Thirty years after the doctor first sat down to think about his goals, he reached his long-term target. But he did it one year at a time. So can you.

This process is really part of your whole life's financial planning—that overarching bigger picture that includes everything from mundane bill paying to wills and estate planning. Because this book is about investment planning, we won't go into as much detail about every goal's moving parts as a total plan would dictate.

What's important for our purposes is to establish goals that are challenging but achievable. I also strongly suggest that you write them down and keep them in a place where you can frequently revisit them. Why? The physical act of writing helps imprint goals on your brain. This is particularly important in this day and age, when we are constantly bombarded with information about stock market action—every minute and every hour.

If your own goals fade you'll end up lost in a sea of data. If the stock market is down for the year and you break even, you'll question whether you won. When it's up 27 percent and you achieved only 15 percent returns, you'll ponder whether you lost. Those are fine questions to ask to help keep things in perspective. But the really important question is, did you meet your own benchmark—your own goals?

Hayden Play:
Be your own benchmark.

Benchmarks like the S&P 500 may hold the public spotlight, but they must be secondary to your personal benchmark. Focus on what returns you reasonably need to meet your goals. Knowing your benchmark can enable you to avoid assuming more risk than necessary. Keep your eye on your game, not the one on the next field.

Element Two: Return Rates—How Fast Can You Drive?

After deciding on the time period you have to reach your goal, the next element of a goal to take into account is your return rate. This is essentially a reasonable assumed rate at which you expect your money to grow in your overall portfolio over an established period of time.

Consider again that 1,000-mile road trip discussed back in Chapter 2. If you need to make that journey in no more than two days to attend your cousin's wedding, you'll have to log an average of 500 miles a day.

The first morning you're golden. Fresh from a good night's sleep in your own bed, you hop in your car, pop in your favorite CD, and you're off on the dry, sunlit road. You drive straight through to noon with no rest stops and no traffic. But a steady downpour starts early in the afternoon. You drive barely 380 miles before collapsing in exhaustion at your hotel. You spend most of the next day speeding and watching your rearview mirror for flashing blue lights.

Yes, you made it to the church on time. But you were so tired once you got there that you could barely keep your eyes open. You didn't have the fun you anticipated at all because you didn't consider just how difficult it might be to drive so far, so fast. You didn't account for the rain.

The rate-of-return element of goal setting is a bit like planning the mileage piece of a road trip. If you're prudent, you'll build in time to account for some bad weather or poor market years. At the same time, while the road or market conditions are right it would be foolish not to push yourself to go as far as you can—even beyond your estimated target—but without doing any dangerous speeding.

Over the years, some of my clients haven't wanted to plan for the rain. They've come in enthused about the high return rates their friends are talking about and excited about conquering the market themselves. Who could blame them in boom years like 1999? More than 100 funds returned more than 100 percent (double your money in a year?!), and at least one was up more than 400 percent. But the bear market of 2000–2002 has brought home the fact that boom times don't last. Only those financial plans that plan for the rain do.

I always try to do my darnedest to make the best out of whatever is happening in the market. But there is a difference between the targeted average return rates you can safely assume you'll get over an extended number of years and what you manage to get in a given year.

When establishing goals five years out or more, four basic ranges can be assumed. A conservative return-rate range is 5 to 6 percent. Moderate would be 7 to 8 percent. Aggressive, in my book, would be any assumed rate of 9 to 10 percent—or more. Of course, to some degree these ranges shift up or down according to the particular cycle of the market we're in. In fact, during real bear markets like the kind in 2000–2002, I ratchet my return rate goals down to what I call a "bunker" level of 3 to 6 percent. In times like these, you're basically aiming to protect your principal. What doesn't change are the labels like conservative, moderate, or aggressive.

I want to stress that these are just examples of rates of return you'll hope to get. There are times when being aggressive gives you a higher rate of return, but there are times when being aggressive gives you disastrous consequences. A higher rate of return usually means you are taking more risk, and higher risk doesn't always mean a higher rate of return. It could turn out just the opposite. The only reason to be aggressive is so you can hold out the hope of higher upside than you'll get with conservative investing.

So, how do you decide what rate to use when determining your return rate goal? As discussed in Chapter 2, part of the equation depends on your psychological risk tolerance. You can get a rough idea of which range to plug yourself into by seeing how you fare on the Risk Quiz. If you're risk averse, you'll shoot for the conservative range, while the risk steady will go the moderate route and the risk seekers might brave 10 percent or above.

The other factors are more quantitative. Traditionally, most people are counseled to take time and their ages into consideration. The important consideration to focus on here is really not age but rather the length of time you have before reaching your goal. The closer you are to needing the money from your investments, the less advisable it would be for you to assume higher risk. That's because the probability of your achieving those higher returns is less likely than your achieving the lower but safer returns. The shorter the time frame, the less predictable the returns are, and the less time you have to make up for any missteps.

Another element that comes into play is income. An engineer earning a $60,000 income simply has less money to invest than a corporate executive who makes $500,000. Because that engineer has less to invest, he also can't afford to take the greater risk that would be necessary to grab that brass ring by putting together an aggressive portfolio with a 10 percent return rate. It's an unfortunate reality of investing: The less money you have, the less you can afford to make a big mistake.

I generally try to steer people to more conservative territory. I haven't always had a lot of company in my camp. The majority of people in the financial industry tend to use 10 percent, a number I consider to be in the aggressive range. But in the throes of the bear market that raged through the years 2000 to 2002, more investors heeded the siren call of prudence. Respected financial thinkers like Warren Buffett are projecting return rates as low as 7 percent over the coming years.[1]

Still, the bottom line on return rates is that nobody can accurately predict them. No matter how hard you work on establishing a realistic goal, you probably won't get the return rate you've picked. I can't emphasize this enough even though I know it's frustrating to hear. After all the work you've put in, how could that be? Because the markets are highly unpredictable. And even the financial industry's best high-tech wizardry has a significant flaw: It is all based on the past.

For example, we know for sure that from 1955 through 2001 you could have earned an average return of about 7.8 percent if you set up a portfolio comprised of about 25 percent stocks, 40 percent bonds, and 35 percent cash, according to Ibbotson's data. What we don't know is how to get that same exact return in the future.

Until we can predict the future—and I don't see that happening anytime soon—that uncertainty will dog us all. That said, I feel fairly confident of these ranges. I've been sticking with them through the many peaks and valleys that the market has tracked over the past three decades. You won't always get what you aim for. But hopefully you won't be too far off.

Elements Three and Four: Putting Numbers on the Dream

Now let's get started on the third and fourth elements—your end goal and how much to invest each year. These calculations are related, so I treat them together.

First, try to write down every large-ticket item you aim to afford in your future. These may include must-haves such as a new car every five years, a home, or college tuition. They could also be desires, such as owning a vacation home. They may be intermediate-term, such as a wish to be a homeowner in 10 years, or long-term, such as a comfortable retirement starting at age 65.

The common denominator is that they all require money and time to accomplish them. Whether you're aiming at a single goal like a home or a more complex one such as retirement, which is really a lifestyle, you'll need to boil it down to a single lump-sum amount of money (Element Three) that you want to have at a given time.

A related issue is your cash flow situation. It's from your monthly (or annual) cash flow that you'll get the money to invest (Element Four) in order to attain your goal. Just as it takes gas to run a car, it also takes a regular and disciplined savings plan to accumulate money in order to execute a game plan.

The Annual Net Worth Checkup

By calculating your net worth, you can determine what progress you're making on your financial goal(s) from year to year.[2] How do you do it? Add up the value of all your assets. This would be the total price that such items as your home, cars, and any stocks, bonds, savings, or other property would have if you sold them today. You then subtract your debts. These would be any mortgages, loans, or credit balances you have outstanding. The final number is your net worth. It's worth remembering. Goals you establish in this chapter will be designed to increase this figure over time. You should check your net worth at least once a year. If it's shrinking, it's time to reassess your game plan. This is just as important to your financial health as that annual physical is to your personal health.

Just how much can you invest? The answer lies in the difference between your incoming cash and your expenses. Budgeting is no fun, but it's the secret to having enough to meet your goals. If you have a problem figuring out how to do this, then buy a budgeting book at your local stationery store. If you use a computer, try using a software program like Quicken.

What you'll need to determine is how much money you can comfortably do without while still covering your and your family's basic needs for shelter, food, transportation, education, life insurance, medical expenses, and emergency stash. (Don't even consider investing unless you've paid off high-interest credit card debt.) And don't forget those costly extras like vacations and second homes. Here you'll need to take some time to examine your checkbook and your priorities. Only then can you figure out how much money you'll have left to invest if you stretched. Once you figure out what's possible to invest monthly you then have all the elements of a workable financial goal.

Walking through a Retirement Goal

All right, you say. You understand there are four basic elements in a goal. But how do they all fit together in real life? I'll use a hypothetical example to illustrate my point. Let's walk through the math that it takes to set a retirement goal for a 45-year-old professor.

Robert is currently earning a salary of $60,000 a year. With his kids preparing to head off to college, Robert is suddenly aware that he is getting older and needs to address his own future needs. Although he's never formally learned about the four elements of a financial goal, he's already got one set: Robert would prefer not to work a day beyond his 65th birthday. He'd like to retire in 20 years (Element One). All the other steps are designed to figure out how or if he can make this wish a reality.

In order to fill in the blanks of all four elements, Robert will next proceed to get a rough idea of what kind of return rate (Element Two) he will aim to get from the investments he will make over the 20 years. He will make this decision after assessing his own psychological risk tolerance using the Risk Quiz in Chapter 2.

Robert has $50,000 already saved, but he is largely depending on his salary to make his investments and cannot afford to take the higher risks associated with an aggressive portfolio. So, given that he also scored a 12 on the Risk Quiz (risk steady but close to the opportunistic investor category), he's looking to build a moderate portfolio that could give him an average annual return rate of 8 percent. So he's got his Element Two—an 8 percent annual expected rate of return—which we'll put aside for a bit while we calculate the mechanics of his saving plan.

When looking ahead to retirement and how much will be needed (Element Three—the lump-sum goal) to live on, you need to use a combination of imagination and common sense. Will your mortgage be paid off? Will you travel more or less? Traditional financial planning suggests you need less to live on in your retirement. I disagree. Modern medicine has tremendously improved the quality of our later years. Some of the seniors I know are going to law school, solo sailing to Bermuda, or treating their children and grandchildren to a family get-together hiking the Alps. Even if you aren't planning an extravagant retirement, it's safe to assume you will need at least as much money to live on in retirement as you have now.

In Robert's case, I might take his current salary and use that as the base. But inflation will reduce the amount that $60,000 will buy in 20 years. To retain the same purchasing power, it's best to factor in inflation.

Inflation Projections

You can get a rough projection of inflation's future impact on any dollar amount by going to www.chicagofed.org/consumerinformation. Click on the interest calculators toolbar and choose the calculator for yearly compound interest. Enter the amount you make now (salary) and 3 percent as the interest rate. Then submit your information. The computer will do the math for you. If you're using just a calculator, you'll need to multiply your principal amount by your projected inflation rate, in this case 3 percent or .03. Then you'll need to do the same with the growing number another 19 times, once for each year you're counting inflation.

How much inflation? We don't know what the next 20 years will bring, but 3 percent is a good assumption to use. So, factoring in inflation, Robert will need $109,000 a year once he retires ($60,000 × 3% compounded over 20 years).

Once we have the annual retirement income target, we need to figure out what other income streams besides investments will be available to fund the goal. In Robert's case, he's expecting to receive $40,000 annually from a pension and $32,000 from Social Security. That leaves $37,000 annually that he'll need to come up with every year from his investments (see Table 3.1). This amount is important, but it's not the same as Element Four, Robert's lump-sum retirement goal. We'll need to do a little more work to get that.

Figuring out exactly the size of the lump sum needed in retirement isn't easy. You quickly bump up against the grisly conundrum of retirement planning: None of us knows how long we're going to live. If you don't know how long you will live, how do you decide how much you need to live on— your ultimate target? How many years will Robert need that $109,000 annual retirement income? In essence you need to back out the final number by using a few simple calculations.

How long your money lasts depends on two variables: the return rate you can get and your withdrawal rate. If you know what kind of portfolio you're going to allocate your money to, you can get some sense of the return rate you can expect. But you can't be certain. In addition, depending on how successful you are at building your nest egg and how much money you'll need in retirement, ratcheting down your withdrawal rate is a choice you can make, but it isn't always a realistic option.

What do I recommend in an ideal world? On this score I'm a dyed-in-the-wool conservative. I like to help my clients save and invest

Table 3.1 **Funding the Goal**

Gross income needed (age 65)	$109,000
Pension (age 65)	–40,000
Social Security (age 65)	–32,000
Annual amount needed from investments	$37,000

enough money to build a nest egg that will allow them to withdraw an amount they can live on comfortably without ever touching or depleting the principal.

As for the kind of return rate I project my clients will get over the long haul, I generally assume 5 to 6 percent a year. But as you can see in Table 3.2 (How Long Will Your Money Last?), a change in either the return rate or the withdrawal rate affects your nest egg's life span. For example, if your money is returning 6 percent and you spent 10 percent of it annually, the nest egg will last 16 years.

But if your money gets a return of 6 percent and you spend only 6 percent annually, it could hypothetically last forever. As a basic rule of thumb, your withdrawal rate must be equal to or below your expected return rate if you don't want to draw down your nest egg and wind up jeopardizing the financial stability of your later retirement years.

To figure out your lump-sum goal, start with 6 percent as your hypothetical withdrawal rate. In my 35 years of experience I've found 6 percent to be a conservative and reliable rate, though some people prefer to be more aggressive and others prefer to be more conservative.

Just divide the amount you'll need every year by 6 percent. In Robert's case that's $37,000 divided by 6% = $616,666. You can see in Table 3.3 that the total lump sum needed is greater for lower withdrawal rates. Though the higher goal may be disconcerting, if you can reduce your withdrawal rate there's the added bonus that you won't need to take as many risks with your investments once you get to retirement because you'll only need, say, a 4 percent return rate to make it last.

So Robert needs a total of $616,666 in total in 20 years. But he doesn't need to start from scratch. Recall, he's already got $50,000 of savings. We will assume that will continue to grow. We can turn to Table 3.4 (How Large Will a Lump Sum Grow?) to look at the impact that the rate of return will have on existing lump-sum investments over the years.

In Robert's case, he has his $50,000 in a moderate portfolio, that could reap 8 percent over the next 20 years. A look at Table 3.4 shows that $1,000 saved now over 20 years at 8 percent compounded return will grow to $4,660.96. Robert can estimate then that his $50,000 will be

Table 3.2 How Long Will Your Money Last?

Annual Withdrawal Rate	Number of Years Your Money Will Last at Return Rate of . . .														
	1%	2%	3%	4%	5%	6%	7%	8%	9%	10%	11%	12%	13%	14%	15%
15%	7	7	8	8	8	9	9	10	11	12	13	14	16	21	Life
14%	7	8	8	9	9	10	10	11	12	13	15	17	22	Life	Life
13%	8	8	9	9	10	11	11	12	14	15	18	23	Life	Life	Life
12%	9	9	10	10	11	12	13	14	16	19	24	Life	Life	Life	Life
11%	10	10	11	12	12	14	16	17	20	25	Life	Life	Life	Life	Life
10%	11	11	12	13	14	16	18	21	27	Life	Life	Life	Life	Life	Life
9%	12	13	14	15	17	19	22	29	Life	Life	Life	Life	Life	Life	Life
8%	13	15	16	18	20	24	31	Life	Life	Life	Life	Life	Life	Life	Life
7%	15	17	19	22	26	33	Life	Life	Life	Life	Life	Life	Life	Life	Life
6%	18	20	23	28	37	Life	Life	Life	Life	Life	Life	Life	Life	Life	Life
5%	22	26	31	41	Life	Life	Life	Life	Life	Life	Life	Life	Life	Life	Life
4%	29	35	47	Life	Life	Life	Life	Life	Life	Life	Life	Life	Life	Life	Life
3%	41	55	Life	Life	Life	Life	Life	Life	Life	Life	Life	Life	Life	Life	Life
2%	70	Life	Life	Life	Life	Life	Life	Life	Life	Life	Life	Life	Life	Life	Life
1%	Life	Life	Life	Life	Life	Life	Life	Life	Life	Life	Life	Life	Life	Life	Life

Table 3.3 The Conservative Approach: A
Withdrawal Rate and Lump Sum That Will Enable
You to Fund the Good Life in Perpetuity

Annual Withdrawal Rate	Lump Sum Needed	Annual Withdrawal Amount
4%	$925,000	$37,000
5%	$740,000	$37,000
6%	$616,666	$37,000
7%	$528,571	$37,000

Table 3.4 How Large Will a Lump Sum Grow? ($1,000 Saved)

Return Rate	5 Years	10 Years	15 Years	20 Years	25 Years	30 Years
5%	$1,276.28	$1,628.89	$2,078.93	$2,653.30	$3,386.35	$4,321.94
6%	$1,338.23	$1,790.85	$2,396.56	$3,207.14	$4,291.87	$5,743.49
7%	$1,402.55	$1,967.15	$2,759.03	$3,869.68	$5,427.43	$7,612.26
8%	$1,469.33	$2,158.92	$3,172.17	$4,660.96	$6,848.48	$10,062.66
9%	$1,538.62	$2,367.36	$3,642.48	$5,604.41	$8,623.08	$13,267.68
10%	$1,610.51	$2,593.74	$4,177.25	$6,727.50	$10,834.71	$17,449.40
11%	$1,685.06	$2,839.42	$4,784.59	$8,062.31	$13,585.46	$22,892.30
12%	$1,762.34	$3,105.85	$5,473.57	$9,646.29	$17,000.06	$29,959.92

$233,048 in two decades (50 × $4,660.96 = $233,048). So he can go back to the lump sum and lop off a good chunk that he won't have to worry about new money for ($616,666 − $233,048 = $383,618). Thus the net amount Robert needs from new money he will invest over the next 20 years is $383,618. As you can see, the more you work with the savings that you already have the more manageable your savings/investment plan can be.

Let's now make the final calculation in this process, using Table 3.5 (How Much Will a Monthly Investment Add Up to in the Long Run?). As you'll recall, Robert is putting together a portfolio that he

Table 3.5   How Much Will a Monthly Investment Add Up to in the Long Run?
($100 Saved Monthly)

Return Rate	60 Months (5 Years)	120 Months (10 Years)	180 Months (15 Years)	240 Months (20 Years)	300 Months (25 Years)	360 Months (30 Years)
5%	$6,800.61	$15,528.23	$26,728.89	$41,103.37	$59,550.97	$83,225.86
6%	$6,977.00	$16,387.93	$29,081.87	$46,204.09	$69,299.40	$100,451.50
7%	$7,159.29	$17,308.48	$31,696.23	$52,092.67	$81,007.17	$121,997.10
8%	$7,347.69	$18,294.60	$34,603.82	$58,902.04	$95,102.64	$149,035.94
9%	$7,542.41	$19,351.43	$37,840.58	$66,788.69	$112,112.19	$183,074.35
10%	$7,743.71	$20,484.50	$41,447.03	$75,936.88	$132,683.34	$226,048.79
11%	$7,951.81	$21,699.81	$45,468.96	$86,563.80	$157,613.33	$280,451.97
12%	$8,166.97	$23,003.87	$49,958.02	$98,925.54	$187,884.66	$349,496.41

hopes will achieve an 8 percent return. So, according to the table, if Robert saves $100 a month at 8 percent annual compounded return, he will have $58,902.04 in 20 years. To figure out how many hundreds of dollars he needs to invest, divide $383,618 by $58,902.04 and then multiply by $100. Robert will need to invest $651.28 a month (Element Four).

There you have it. Robert has figured out the four pieces to his goal puzzle: (1) 20 years at (2) 8 percent in order to have (3) a lump sum of $383,618 by investing (4) $651.28 monthly.

This example is about the easiest approach you could take to mapping out a goal by just using a calculator and some simple tables. If you don't do anything else, do this. It will enable you to consistently save and invest money with a commonsense game plan.

What's Good about Planning for Retirement This Way?

- It will give you a relatively simple way to target a goal if you are doing it yourself without the help of a computer or planner.
- It will give you specific sums of money to target for saving/investing each month and year.

What's Not So Good about Planning This Way?

- It doesn't take into consideration taxes. These have a significant impact during the growth years as well as the withdrawal years.
- It doesn't take into consideration the impact of inflation during the years you are withdrawing money. At 3 percent inflation you would need twice as much money in 24 years. This is a serious shortcoming of the "do it by hand" approach. Although we took inflation into account when figuring out what the equivalent of $60,000 now will be in 20 years ($109,000), we didn't consider its effect after the first day of retirement. In other words, inflation keeps affecting what you can buy with what the nest egg is producing.
- It doesn't take into consideration the fluctuating return on your investments from year to year. The only way to work with that kind of projection is to use the "Monte Carlo" method that I will discuss later in the chapter. Even then, you are only working with the probability of a particular investment scenario working out. Realistically, you must closely monitor your investment game plan year by year and make adjustments to your game plan as necessary.

Getting Some Help

For the reasons outlined earlier, Robert's example is a good way to plan for retirement, but it has its pitfalls. I suggest you also consider either using web sites or working with a Certified Financial Planner.

Part of the challenge in defining goals is that there are many variables and precious few assumptions that can be trusted. If you are working with an advisor, then he or she will work through how taxes, inflation, and interest-rate fluctuations may affect your portfolio. Or, if you're a do-it-yourselfer, there are a number of web sites and affordable software programs that can help you with calculations, such as the Quicken.com retirement planner and SmartMoney.com's retirement worksheets. In either case, there are no guarantees. But it's extremely important to have an idea of where you're going.

Strategizing for Bear Market Retirees:
The Hayden Fence

So you just retired into one of the worst routs in stock market history? What's a conservative investor to do? Lots. I've received a tremendous number of calls on this issue. I've advised many clients to take the steps outlined next to protect themselves. My strategy assumes that it will take three years for the S&P 500 Index (and your portfolio) to go through a full down cycle and return to the levels it started at—to break even. Here's how it works in a nutshell (assuming accidents and health problems are covered by the necessary insurance):

1. Put a year's worth of income in a money market fund (to live on).
2. Take two years' worth of income and invest it in a short-term bond fund. Returns here should not vary much even in a falling market.
3. Take the balance of your nest egg and put it into a well-diversified stock and bond portfolio with a proper balance between offense and defense. (More on offense and defense in Chapter 5.)
4. At the beginning of each bear market year, you'll replenish your money market fund by replacing that outlay with money from your short-term bond fund. This will give you steady income for three years.

This system aims to provide an income for three years no matter what happens in the market—so you don't have to touch your portfolio when it's down. If the market is up you can simply replenish your bond fund annually with money from your portfolio. This approach also gives your portfolio time to recover.

Outside assistance is particularly helpful if you are trying to work through a long-term plan with multiple goals. For example, if you are ambitiously working on a 30-year plan you will quickly notice that all of your goals do not come due magically in 30 years. You want the money for that dream house on the lake when you're 45, not 55. Your kids need braces when they need them, not when you can afford them. Working through the variables with a computer program or an advisor can help point out whether or not the goals are realistic.

What in the World Is Monte Carlo?

One fairly new concept in goal planning is Monte Carlo Simulation (MCS). No, we're not talking about the gambling mecca. Monte Carlo Simulation is a methodology originally used by statisticians, actuaries, and engineers that offers a statistical assessment of whether you'll be able to meet your retirement goals.

What Monte Carlo Simulation does is attempt to model thousands of random markets and time periods and their potential effect on your goals. For example, you and I know that in real life you can't expect the market to give you the same return rates year after year. And obviously no one knows how long he or she will live. This sophisticated software takes all these variables into account. It then gives an answer in percentage form that quantifies the probability of achieving your goal.

Let's walk through how this works using The Portfolio Survival Simulator, which employs MCS. You can download the software off the Web for a small fee (www.portfoliosurvival.com). Let's assume you've just retired at age 65 with $1 million already saved. You get $4,000 monthly from your pension and $2,000 from Social Security benefits. You're still very active, and you'd like to withdraw $12,000 from your investments each month for the next 20 years. But you figure your lifestyle will slow down a bit after that, for the following 10 years you plan to withdraw only $7,000 a month.

Once you enter all these numbers into the Portfolio Survival software, you find this plan will deplete your nest egg too quickly for your comfort. Depending on how you decide to invest your money, the software suggests that your portfolio has only a 13 percent chance of surviving for 30 years. But time's on your side. Using the software, you can tinker with your plan to boost your portfolio's survivability. You do this by lowering your goal, reducing your withdrawal rates, or reworking how you've allocated your investments (stocks, bonds, and cash). For example, by reducing the drawdown rate to $9,000 monthly in the first 20 years and $5,000 monthly in the next 10, the probability of the portfolio surviving rises to 73 percent.

Recently a handful of financial planners have started using Monte Carlo because they believe it offers the most sophisticated and realistic retirement planning available. In addition to The Portfolio Survival Simulator just discussed, it's also the methodology behind retirement calculation web sites offered by Financial Engines (www.financialengines.com) and T. Rowe Price (www.troweprice.com).

Step 3, Know Your Goals: Summing Up

Setting goals is a complex task that's part art, part science. But you're on your way if you understand the four basic elements that make up a solid goal. They include (1) the time period over which you will invest and assume (2) a specified annual rate of return, with the aim of reaching (3) a lump-sum goal by saving (4) a given amount regularly. It may help for you to use the following questions, along with the tables and information outlined in this chapter, to get started. Once you've developed a goal, move on to the next chapter and we'll begin figuring out how to build a portfolio or strategy to make it all happen.

1. Define your life financial goals. (Write them down on paper.)
2. What are the benefits of reaching it? (This will encourage you to remain committed.)
3. How much money do you need to reach your goal, and by when?
4. How much money do you need to save each:

   Week?
   Month?
   Year?

5. What rate of return can you realistically hope to get?
6. Can you use an IRA (regular or Roth), 401(k), 403(b), or SEP IRA to help reach this goal?
7. What savings/investments will you use?

Chapter 4

Step 4: Get the Fund Fever

So far we've assessed where you'd like to end up financially, and your risk constitution for getting there. The steps we've taken to date have led you to better understand how fast you can reasonably hope to get where you want to go.

Now it's time to develop a sound strategy to help ensure you get there. In Chapters 5, 6, and 7, I discuss how to allocate among asset classes, fund styles, and specific mutual funds to achieve your goals. I offer several alternatives, but they all have one common theme: They rely on mutual funds. Mutual funds are my tool of choice for investing. In this chapter, I describe why.

Stocks and Bonds: A Primer

First, a quick refresher on stocks and bonds, and then on to mutual funds. What is a stock? Shares of stock are issued by corporations. Buying a stock share means you actually own a piece of a company. Let's imagine you organized a corporation for the purpose of buying a car wash. You sold one share of common stock apiece to nine people at

$100 per share and kept one share for yourself at $100. By doing this, you would have capitalized your corporation at $1,000, and it would have 10 shareholders.

Each shareholder has a partial ownership in your car wash corporation. They took what is called an equity position and will participate in the future gains or losses of the corporation as long as they own shares. If your company has real earnings and a good growth pattern, it will ideally pay the stockholders a dividend, or a share of the profits, over the long term.

In the short term, the price of any stock can be affected by behavior of the market. For instance, an entire sector of the market could be down and, regardless of how healthy that company is, the price of the stock could go down. For example, when the entire tech sector fell out of favor, the price of IBM stock dropped from about $133 a share in August 2000 to about $76 in May 2002. A price of $76 was arguably too low based on an analysis of the solid business IBM was doing. This is a case where movement in an entire sector as well as the entire market affected the price of the stock. In the longer term—a two-to-five-year time span—the price of stock will be determined more by the earnings of the company.

When I think about the lack of predictability of stocks, I'm reminded of some famous advice that the cowboy-turned-philosopher Will Rogers once gave. "Don't gamble, take all your savings and buy some good stock," he advised. "Hold it till it goes up, then sell it. If it don't go up . . . don't buy it."[1] Will Rogers reminds me that there's no such thing as a sure bet or a guaranteed rise in stock prices—and helps me keep my sense of humor.

Now let's examine bonds. A separate and distinct asset class from stocks, bonds are considered debt instruments. They are essentially IOUs to the people investing in them. Remember that car wash corporation that issued stock? Now let's assume that the car wash also wants to borrow some money.

Instead of going to the bank, it decides to borrow the money from individuals. If it wanted to borrow $100,000 from 10 individuals, it would create 10 bonds worth $10,000 each. In order to attract people who will loan it the money, the company generally has to offer to pay a higher rate of interest than is otherwise available. Since guaranteed bonds issued by the U.S. government may pay about 5.5 percent, your car wash will need to pay bondholders at least, say, 8 percent to encourage people to buy its bonds despite the increased risk a company poses over that of the U.S. government.

People who are going to loan the corporation $10,000 don't want to wait indefinitely to get their money back. So the car wash decides to have the bonds "mature" in 10 years. That is when the investors will get their money back. The car wash bond investor will essentially be making a loan of $10,000 by buying a 10-year $10,000 bond. Each year the bondholder will be paid interest of 8 percent—$800 a year. The bond is guaranteed by the corporation. As long as the corporation is financially sound, the investors have a reasonable assurance they will get their principal back.

It sounds simple—a guaranteed loan for 10 years at a nice rate of interest. That appears to make it a safer investment than the stock in the same company. But while bonds are considered to be lower on the risk-scale than stocks, they are not risk free.

Why? Let's say in the third year, Uncle John—one of the $10,000 bondholders—gets sick and needs the money. At that point, he will be forced to sell it at the market price.

There are a number of variables that determine the price Uncle John will get for his bond. One of the key elements is the relationship between a bond's interest rate and the interest rate of new bonds in the existing market.

It boils down to this: If interest rates rise above the level at which Uncle John bought his bond, Uncle John will probably get less than the $10,000 he paid if he must sell it before it matures. If interest rates fall, Uncle John may be able to sell his bond at a premium, getting more than he paid for it originally. (This is the old playground teeter-totter analogy: When interest rates go up, existing bond values go down, and when interest rates go down, existing bond values go up.)

Why does it work this way? Say interest rates have gone up from 8 per-cent to 9 percent. The value of Uncle John's bond needs to compensate a new investor for the higher yield that he or she could reap from a new $10,000 bond pegged to the higher 9 percent interest rate (which would pay $900 annually) rather than Uncle John's bond's 8 percent (which pays $800 annually).

If Uncle John decides to sell his bond at the end of the third year, we know there are seven remaining years when Uncle John's bond will pay $100 less than what an investor would get from a new bond. So Uncle John may get only about $9,300 for the bond. That's the original bond price ($10,000) less the loss of $100 in additional interest over seven years ($700).

However, Uncle John could luck out. Let's say interest rates have fallen to 7 percent and a comparable $10,000 bond yields only $700 a year, or $100 less than Uncle John's bond pays. In that case Uncle John may be able to sell his bond for somewhere in the neighborhood of $10,700. That's the original bond price ($10,000) plus $700 to account for the additional $100 in interest Uncle John's bond will offer over seven years.

Of course we have greatly simplified this matter for illustration pur-poses. Bond prices are affected by a great many other factors, such as infla-tion and the length of time to maturity. For example, the longer the time before the new investor can get his or her money back (maturity date), the more the bond is discounted. The bond industry uses voluminous tables and high-tech calculators to sort out all the variables that go into pricing. But what's important to remember is this: There's no such thing as a free lunch. There's also no such thing as a risk-free investment, even in bonds.

Funds versus Stocks: The Advantages

Now on to mutual funds. A mutual fund essentially is a basket of stocks (or a basket of bonds, or both). Instead of buying stocks or bonds, which represent ownership in or a loan to a single company, you buy shares in a fund. The fund's manager or management team in turn buys many, many stocks or bonds. That's where you get your di-versification. (For the purposes of simplifying this comparison, we will compare stock funds to stocks. But bond funds share many of the same advantages over bonds.)

With a mutual fund, you instantly have exposure to lots of stocks, and someone else—the fund manager—makes all the buy/sell decisions. If any one stock tanks, it eats up only a little bit of the money you invested. That minimizes your risk.

There are many reasons that investing experts and the mutual fund industry tout mutual funds over stocks for individual investors. For me, it basically comes down to this: Funds are safer. If you want diversification and the relative safety that comes with it, it's easier to get that by choosing funds rather than by building a portfolio stock by stock.

Here are a few reasons why.

Stock Picking Is Tough Stuff

Fund buyers don't have to pick stocks. That's a welcome relief, because successful stock picking is a tall order. If you've tried it, you've probably learned this yourself. If you haven't already discovered how difficult successful stock picking is from your own experience, then you need only look at the track record of the majority of mutual fund managers in this country (who get *paid* to pick stocks) to reach the same conclusion. By and large their record is not good, which is not that surprising: It's extremely tough to find a winning stock, to buy it low and to sell it high.

Do the names Sunbeam, Global Crossing, or Enron sound familiar? These are all companies that once were adored by investors—both novices and even some experts—but some ended up in bankruptcy court thanks to accounting problems and related alleged misdeeds. Their downfalls whacked investors who thought they were doing the smart thing by buying shares in these once widely respected outfits.

And it's not just bad apples that tank. There are plenty of examples of less infamous but equally steep declines. How many people bought Cisco Systems at $70 when they thought the networking giant was invincible, only to see its stock price drop steadily following the tech wreck that began in March 2000 to $11.04, after the terrorist attacks in

September 2001 and lower still, to $8.12 in October 2002? Or how about America Online, which was as high as $95.81 shortly before it agreed to purchase "old" media company Time Warner? Two and a half years later it had lost 82 percent of its value. Then there's General Electric, perhaps the closest anyone thought they could come to a sure thing. Its value was cut in half between August 2000 and April 2002.

I point out these stock stories not because stock picking is impossible, but because it's very difficult. I'm in the business, and I don't pick stocks for myself. Nor would I hire just anyone to do it for me. Many professionals don't succeed at stock picking. Robert Olstein, manager of the Olstein Financial Alert fund, is one of the managers who has beat the S&P 500 Index in recent years, putting up double-digit returns every full year for the six years after his fund launched in 1996, even in 2000 and 2001 when the broader market lost ground. Yet while Olstein has a great record, not every stock pick is a winner.

Finding one of those better stock pickers like Olstein is the subject of Chapter 6. It's not a breeze, but it's easier than picking stocks yourself— and less risky, which brings me to my next point.

You Can Manage Risk More Easily with Funds

There are two main kinds of risks you encounter with the stock market (and again, the same goes for the bond market): market risk and specific investment risk. Market risk is the risk that the whole market takes a turn for the worse, thanks to, say, a recession, oil crisis, high interest rates, or war. The only real way to protect against market risk is to keep at least some of your money out of the market. That's a concept discussed in Chapter 2.

The second risk is specific investment risk. Specific investment risk is the risk that the stock you own will deflate or blow up due to its own problems. The analogous risk in a fund is that the returns in your particular fund will plummet: The market does fine, but your fund doesn't.

With both stocks and funds, quantitative metrics can help you size up specific investment risk. A stock's "beta," for example, measures its sensitivity to a certain market benchmark like the S&P 500 stock market index. It indicates how far a stock has moved, historically, compared with the S&P, which has a beta of 1. If a stock has a beta of 1.3, it's likely to move 30 percent more, higher or lower, than the S&P's move. A beta below 1 means a stock has been less volatile than the index. Likewise, a fund also has a beta based on the weighted average beta of its stock holdings.

These measurements are based on historical data. They are an attempt to predict the future based on the past. But because the future is unpredictable, they aren't always right. Things go wrong.

No matter how reliably a stock behaved in the past, it can still crumble. No business—and that's what you're buying when you buy stocks—is a sure thing. A lousy CEO, a crooked accountant, an incredible competitor all can mean the demise of a once viable company.

Equity mutual funds, in contrast, hold many stocks. In fact, this diversification is required by law. The Investment Company Act of 1940 provides that a diversified mutual fund, for at least 75 percent of its assets, may not make purchases that cause more than 5 percent of the fund's total assets to be in any one company or that cause the fund to own more than 10 percent of the outstanding voting shares of any one company.

Because of this, investors can greatly minimize specific investment risk through funds. If a fund has 100 stocks and five tank, those tankers can only have so much of an impact on the total returns. Ninety-five positions that do better balance out the five losers.

For example, if you wanted to invest in health-care companies from January 1997 through April 2002, you could have spread your risk by putting your money in the Vanguard Health Care fund rather than a specific pharmaceutical company. During that period, Bristol-Myers Squibb rose a paltry 7 percent while Pfizer nearly doubled. But if you were in the Vanguard fund instead, you hedged your risk. Not to mention the fact that the Vanguard fund had a cumulative return of 190.73 percent during that same time—better return, less risk.

All this doesn't make funds risk free. A manager, for example, might buy lots of stocks in a risky sector. But that's a risk you can prepare for—a risk you can manage. You can look at the fund manager's historical record, the types of stocks he or she has bought, the kinds of swings the portfolio has experienced over time. You would also learn that sector funds (or what I like to call special teams that are actually funds focused on a specific industry) can be very dangerous and should be kept to a minimum in your portfolio.

If you study this historical data, you can grasp your real potential downside loss. And you can decide whether you're prepared to handle it. If the fund has had fairly consistent returns over several years, the odds of an out-and-out blowup of the entire fund are lower than for the same thing happening with one stock. Unless the fund management has a sudden shift in style—and that's something you can pick up on if you monitor your investments—you'll have a much better chance of avoiding a whacking with funds than with owning a few individual stocks or bonds.

You'll Have Less Paperwork Angst

Funds have their share of paperwork but stocks can be even more of a hassle. Whether it's tracking your purchase or sale price, moving shares between brokerage firms, or filling out your Schedule D tax form, stocks are a pain. And the more of a pain investing is, the less likely you'll do it well. I believe in keeping things simple whenever possible. Funds help keep investing simple.

As with stocks, there's no shortage of information available on mutual funds. You can look up the performance of your fund in newspapers, in magazines, and on the Internet.

Finally, as with stocks, there is a public market for the funds and they can readily be bought and sold. You can even arrange regular fund withdrawals easily. For instance, instead of reinvesting dividends or interest, you can have them paid to you. You can also instruct a fund to send you a given percentage of its value—such as 5 percent a year or $200 a month. Of course, these determinations should be based on a careful assessment of your goals.

Both Large and Small Investors Can Benefit from Funds

The instant diversification that funds offer is available (and perhaps even more important to you) if you have only small amounts of money to invest. Whether you invest \$500 or \$5,000 in any one fund, you still get the benefit of owning a basket rather than putting all your money in one of the eggs in that basket. Thanks partly to commissions, even today's low ones, it would be tough to achieve that diversification by buying individual stocks.

Alternately, if you have large sums of money to invest, you can opt to invest that money in different funds rather than have two or three money managers. It can be awkward or unpleasant to "fire" personal managers. It's easy to get in and out of mutual funds, which are liquid and can be readily bought and sold.

Still not convinced that funds offer a safer and more diversified investment alternative to stocks? Then consider what happened as the markets spiraled downward during the first six months of 2002. As you can see in Table 4.1, the most widely held stocks posted much poorer returns than the most widely held funds.

The lefthand columns show how the 10 most popular stocks performed from January 2, 2002, through June 30, 2002. (The stocks were owned by the largest number of accounts at Merrill Lynch.) The righthand columns show the performance of the most widely held stock funds over the same period. (The funds have more money invested in them than any other stock funds, according to Morningstar.)

Remember this was the Great Bear Market and there were relatively few ports in the storm. In fact, only one of these widely held investments returned a profit. Which one, you ask? You guessed it: It was a fund, the Pimco Institutional Total Return.

Funds versus Stocks

- Fund picking is hard, but stock picking is harder.
- Funds can be risky, but stocks are generally riskier.
- Funds have some paperwork, but stocks have more.
- Funds give small investors instant diversification that's more difficult to achieve with stocks.

Table 4.1   **Beating the Bear: Funds Offer Some Shelter from the Storm**

Stock	Performance from January 2 through June 30, 2002		Mutual Fund
Lucent	−67.7%	−15.6%	American A Growth Fund of America
Avaya	−59.3	−14.6	Fidelity Magellan
AT&T Wireless	−59.3	−13.2	Vanguard Index 500
AOL Time Warner	−54.2	−9.7	Fidelity Growth & Income
EMC Corporation	−43.8	−7.2	American A Invest Co. of America
Intel	−41.9	−6.9	American A New Perspect
AT&T	−41.0	−4.0	American A WA Mutual
IBM	−40.5	−2.8	American A Europacific Growth
Oracle	−31.4	−0.9	Fidelity Contrafund
Home Depot	−28.0	+4.0	Pimco Institutional Total Return

Note: While this chart appears to bear out the theory that funds are generally less volatile than stocks, there is no guarantee or assurance of future performance.
Stock information source: Associated Press (courtesy of AP/Wide World Photos). *Fund information source:* Morningstar.

Over this period stocks clearly took a bigger whacking. The worst of the most popular stocks was down 67.7 percent while the worst of the most widely held funds fell only 15.6 percent. Which group would you rather have been in? If you still pick stocks, I say you've picked your poison.

The Downside of Funds

Are funds perfect? No. Like anything else in life, a good fund is a great deal, and a bad fund is a raw deal. And there *are* bad funds. If a manager consistently fails to beat the fund's benchmark and doesn't reduce investors' risk, the fund is a bad deal. If a manager generates enormous tax liability for investors that eats up decent returns, the fund can be a bad deal. If a fund pairs high expense ratios with low returns, that's a bad deal.

In addition, there are some inherent disadvantages that come with funds that you wouldn't have to address if you stuck with stocks. Despite these, I'd still choose funds any day, but I think it's wise to understand the potential drawbacks. They include:

- Tax impact.
- Management costs.
- Fund size.
- Purchase and sale timing.

Tax Impact

Under investment law, funds must distribute any gains they have to the investor each year. That means you could have a short- or long-term capital gain on which you would have to pay tax. That said, many managers have recently become more tax conscious and are trying to offset gains and losses within a fund, thereby reducing the tax burden. As of this writing, there is pending legislation to reduce the tax burden on funds. If it becomes a law, then some of the gains would not be taxed until the investor actually sells the shares in fund.

Management Costs

Excessive management costs could be a disadvantage to owning a fund. The average expense ratio for an equity mutual fund was about 1.4 percent at the end of 2002, according to Morningstar. (The annual expense ratio is described by Morningstar as the percentage of a fund's assets that is deducted each year to cover such expenses as administrative and operating costs.) I think even this is too high and needs to be reduced, but I still like funds. You can educate yourself about costs and pick your funds accordingly. Two fund families noted for low annual costs are Vanguard and American Funds. When taking costs into consideration, don't confuse the annual management fee with a load. There's a difference. For instance, American Funds have a load, but the annual management fee is much lower than that of most funds. I will discuss load funds in Chapter 6, but suffice it to say that I don't believe a load fund is in and of itself a disadvantage.

Fund Size

Sometimes a fund becomes so large and has so much money to invest that its flexibility is reduced. This can become a disadvantage to investors in that fund. The greatest concern about size generally relates to funds that invest in small companies, because only so many good small companies exist. A manager of a fund that invests in such companies could run out of options and be forced to start investing in larger companies. Since that is not really the market segment that the manager is experienced in, the fund's performance could suffer.

Purchase and Sale Timing

Unlike stocks, you cannot buy or sell funds in the middle of the day. When you invest in a fund you get the price at the end of the trading day. Likewise, when you sell you get out at the end of the trading day. The fact that you don't know exactly what price you'll be selling at until the end of the day means you could get a higher price or a lower price than was in effect at the time you placed your buy or sell order. Generally, this is not a significant problem, particularly for long-term investors.

Poor performance, taxes, costs and reduced flexibility. These are real issues with funds. But they don't mean that the entire fund industry is a scam. Rather, I urge you to take these factors into consideration when you choose funds.

There is one downside of funds, though, that can't be avoided by fund choice. That's the fun factor. Some folks just find funds dull. They crave the thrill of stocks. And to a certain extent that's understandable. While individual stocks carry enormous risk, they can also hold out the hope of enormous potential upside. Huge upside—the proverbial killing—is a lot tougher to get with a broadly diversified mutual fund where assets are spread out. Remember that fund that held 100 stocks? If five do incredibly well, their gains can only have so much of an impact on the total returns. The 95 other positions that are good, fair, or lousy balance out the big winners.

But by now you know my theory on this: Fulfill your thrill cravings in Vegas. The goal with successful investing is consistent returns that build over time, not one-hit wonders. If you really need to satisfy your hankering for excitement in the stock market, set aside a small trading kitty—no more than 5 percent of your whole portfolio, preferably 1 to 2 percent. Then trade and trade and trade that to your heart's content. For the rest, stick with funds.

The Many Faces of Funds

Avoiding direct investments in stocks or bonds is one of the main ways to assure a diversified portfolio. The second way is to pick funds of varied asset classes and styles to provide protection from market swings.

There are three basic asset classes: stocks, bonds, and cash. For our purposes, since we're focusing on funds, the asset classes are stock mutual funds, bond mutual funds, and money market mutual funds. Because the underlying securities behave differently, the funds bring a range of advantages and disadvantages to your portfolio. The process of allocating to these three asset classes will determine how successful you are at reaching your goals.

Stock Mutual Funds

As mentioned earlier, stock mutual funds invest in stocks of companies. A good stock mutual fund gives you the opportunity to cash in on the economy without taking a risk on any one company. Stock funds are typically the growth engine of a portfolio. They provide the best opportunity to keep up with inflation. This is because they invest in companies that offset the effect of rising prices by increasing what they charge for goods and services. Of the three fund asset classes, stock funds historically offer the highest return but also pose the greatest risk.

Bond Mutual Funds

Bond funds offer more security to a portfolio than stock funds. This is because of that guaranteed interest rate that companies pay bondholders over the term of the bond—that is, so long as the company remains solvent. This set return is why bond funds are considered an important stabilizer for a portfolio.

Although the bond fund's fixed-income stream causes it to be considered a lower-risk investment than stock funds, it is by no means a no-risk investment. To get that annual return, the lender must remain healthy and solvent. The risk of that company defaulting is real. And rising interest rates could cut into the value of your bond fund's investment—meaning a decline in your principal.

Money Market Mutual Funds

Money market funds have even less risk, and less upside, than bond funds. Essentially like cash, these relatively stable funds invest in short-term obligations of governments and corporations, such as U.S. Treasury bills and certificates of deposit. Portfolios often rely on money market funds as a hedge against the stock market's volatility as well as

---

Getting to Know Your Fund's Investment Philosophy

I use the style terminology of Morningstar, the Chicago-based company that is a leader in fund research and analysis. A manager may not agree with the style designation he or she is assigned by Morningstar. The way I feel fully confident in the tags is by talking with the manager or reading about him or her in the voluminous mutual fund press. You can achieve the same by doing an Internet search on the manager (with Google, for example); checking news on web sites like Morningstar (www.morningstar.com) or TheStreet.com (www.thestreet.com); reading fund literature; or placing a call to the fund's customer service line.

for cash flow purposes. You often can write checks on your money in such a fund even while you are earning a better interest rate than you would if the money were in a passbook savings account. Most of all, while money market funds are not Federal Deposit Insurance Corporation (FDIC) insured, they are as close as you can get to total safety while usually earning a tiny bit more interest than in a bank savings account. This is a good place for money to sit on the sidelines while you are waiting for investment opportunities.

Stock Fund Investment Styles: The Subsets

For the stock asset classes, funds can be broken down into smaller categories that relate to style. For general U.S. equity funds (not including international funds and sector funds like technology or health) a fund style consists of two main components. These are size (small-cap, mid-cap, large-cap funds) and the investment philosophy of the manager (value, growth, and blend).

When you look at the composite picture, you end up with nine different styles that have varied levels of risk and opportunity as illustrated in the Morningstar equity style box (see Table 4.2). They range from large-cap value funds, which are considered the safest pure equity funds, to small-cap growth, which are the riskiest.

If you're at all a student of the mutual fund industry, you've heard these labels before. At best, these tags attempt to help investors understand what they're getting with a fund so they can properly diversify their portfolios. At worst, they can be rigid fences that box in an investor—or a manager—just when rugged market conditions warrant agility.

Size

The standard measure of company size is what is called its market capitalization. This number is reached by multiplying the current share price (the current price at which investors are valuing the company) by the number of outstanding shares. For example, a company with 100 million shares outstanding at a $15 price has a market cap of $1.5 billion.

Table 4.2 Morningstar Equity Style Box

	Value	Blend	Growth
Large			
Medium			
Small			

Source: Morningstar.

Just how that kind of number stacks up depends on the economic times. For example, until late 1998 Morningstar classified companies as small-cap if they were valued at $1 billion or less and as large-cap if they were valued at $5 billion or more. Those in between were mid-cap. But those break points lost their significance as the raging bull market inflated stock prices in the 1990s.

As a result, in 1998 Morningstar decided on a new classification system. It now defines the large-cap category as the top 5 percent of 5,000 U.S. stocks, the mid-cap as the next 15 percent, and the small-cap as the remaining 80 percent of companies. As of early 2002, that meant that any fund investing in companies valued at under $1.29 billion was considered small-cap while those investing in firms above $8.61 billion were large-cap and anything in between was mid-cap.

Generally it's good to have some of each of three sizes of funds at any given time to protect yourself as they swing in and out of favor. Market preferences for company size change over time, affecting the stock's value to the investor. Such a shift from large caps to small caps occurred from the beginning of 1998 through the spring of 2002.

From January 1998 through December 1999 the S&P 500 Index, comprised of large-cap companies, had an annualized return of 24.75 percent, while the Russell 2000 index, containing mostly small-cap stocks, had an annualized return of 8.70 percent. The tables turned from January 2000 through April 2002. During that period the S&P 500 posted a negative annualized return of 11.37 percent compared with a positive 1.82 percent performance by the Russell 2000.

Investment Philosophy

The second component of style is investment philosophy. There are three main approaches: value, growth, and a value/growth blend.

Value

Value fund managers are bargain hunters. They always want to buy a dollar's worth of something for 50 cents and watch it grow to a dollar. The general way value managers approach investing is to analyze a company, decide what the intrinsic value of the company is—what it would be worth if it were sold off at a given point in time—and then buy the stock only if it is trading at a significant discount to that value.

Value managers are often thought of as contrarians because the cheap stocks they buy almost by definition are the ones others don't like. The father of value investing is generally considered to be the late Columbia University professor Benjamin Graham. In the classic investing book *Security Analysis*, Benjamin Graham and coauthor David Dodd encouraged investors to consider the intrinsic value of a company before investing in it. Important elements to consider, they maintained, included the company's value as an ongoing concern, its business type, and the general business climate. "Without some defined standards of value for judging whether securities are over- or under-priced in the market-place, the analyst is a potential victim of the tides of pessimism and euphoria which sweep the security markets," Graham and Dodd wrote. "Equally destructive of satisfactory investment are the fads and herd instincts of major participants in the market-place."[2]

Value investors like Warren Buffett (the only student to whom Graham awarded an A+ at Columbia) pay close attention to where a stock's price is compared with the company's fundamentals—particularly its excess cash flow—and compared with what return they could expect on the stock. Basically, they like to buy into out-of-favor companies that they believe have the potential for turnaround.

Value managers are often scorned during hypergrowth periods for their conservatism. One of my favorite value managers is Jean-Marie Eveillard of the infamous First Eagle SoGen Global fund. He was scorned in 1998 when his fund was down 0.3 percent while tech was building its bubble. He had the last laugh when the bubble burst.

Growth

So-called growth managers pay less attention to what a stock should be valued at now than what they think it will be later. Even if a company is trading at a very high price compared to its historical earnings or future earnings expectations, if the growth investor senses momentum in the stock price, he or she will buy it.

Still, for a fund manager to decide that a company is a good growth play, most look for a record of long-term growth in earnings and a conviction that the growth will continue in the future. The tech stocks, particularly Internet stocks, that zoomed in the bull market of 1998–1999, by and large did not represent companies with real earnings growth potential. Despite the fact that several companies had no earnings, they were soaring like rockets in a cloudless sky. That is not the serious growth that good growth managers want.

Solid growth managers like Spiros Segalas of Harbor Capital Appreciation look for real earnings growth and a stock that is appropriately valued in comparison to the company's rate of earnings growth. They are not looking for a discounted deal, but rather a fair deal in a continuing growth pattern.

Blend

A blend fund combines both value and growth stocks in the same portfolio. These managers have more flexibility to allocate their investments to different styles at different times. They generally will buy a stock on a value basis but they will continue to hold onto that stock even when it crosses the threshold and becomes a growth stock. What you've got with blend manager is someone who can respond to market cycles.

In fact, some of my favorite managers' philosophies are really outgrowths of the "blend" category. I call them "freestyle" managers. These are managers who, in the spirit of some of the first fund managers 40 years ago, make all the allocation decisions within their own funds. Their main objective is to buy a stock at the right price—and see it grow—no matter what the category the stock is in. They defy categorization, moving easily from small cap to large, value to growth—wherever they believe they can achieve performance in the market at the time.

Some examples, and these are folks I profile in Chapter 8, include Bill Fries and Bob Olstein. What I like about these managers, besides their outstanding long-term numbers, is that they do not blame the market for their performance woes. They'll never say "My style is out of style"—because they don't have a strict industry-generated style. They might have a bad run, but they'll take responsibility for it and try to do what it takes to improve in the moment.

If I could rely solely on freestyle managers, I probably would. But today there just aren't that many good ones. That stems in part from some systemic changes in the fund industry. Two or three mutual funds no longer constitute a person's whole investment portfolio. Instead, each fund is designed to fit a particular and very specific investment style. As a result, most mutual fund managers are forced to fit themselves into narrow categories of style that have a well-defined discipline. They cut their teeth in a value shop or a growth shop, a small-cap shop or a large-cap blue-chip shop, and that's what they know.

That kind of expertise isn't always a bad thing. Some of my favorite managers are careful to remain consistent with their style. But it means an investor needs to pick enough mutual funds to get exposure to different parts of the market. It's extremely important for investors to be aware of the heightened responsibility they now have to make sure their investments are allocated properly. Many managers these days assume that investors are taking steps on their own to spread out their risks among different investments in order to protect themselves. In other words, to a great extent the allocation decision has shifted away from the fund manager to the investor.

Bond Fund Investment Styles: The Subsets

Because bonds behave differently than stocks, bond asset funds are broken down into their own particular smaller categories that relate to style. Bond fund styles essentially have two main components.

These are average duration, which is a measure of the fund's interest-rate sensitivity (short, intermediate, and long), and credit quality (low, moderate, and high). Credit quality measures the financial health of the bond-issuing entity and its ability to pay back the bond.

When you look at the composite picture, you end up with nine different bond fund styles, as illustrated by the Morningstar fixed-income style-box grid (see Table 4.3). The lowest-risk bond fund would be a short-term, high-quality style while the highest-risk bond would be a long-duration, low-quality fund.

Table 4.3   **Morningstar Fixed-Income Style Box**

	Short	Intermediate	Long
High			
Medium			
Low			

Source: Morningstar.

Interest-Rate Sensitivity

Short, intermediate, and long are the terms used to describe just how volatile a particular bond fund's portfolio might be in relation to the threat of fluctuating interest rates. They are useful labels because they help investors differentiate among funds. To determine where a bond fund fits along this risk spectrum, Morningstar looks at an abstract figure known as a fund's average duration (this is calculated by fund companies).

Although duration is also expressed as a number of years, it should not be confused with a bond's maturity date. Maturity is the set length of time until the bondholder's principal must be paid back. By contrast, duration is considered by Morningstar to be a more accurate measure of risk than maturity because it takes into account factors in addition to maturity, including the risk that interest rates will rise and drive down bond prices.

Generally, long-term bond funds with higher average durations are considered more risky, in part because there's more time for interest rates to rise above the level that the bonds were bought at. If you want less volatility and nearly as much return, stick with short- and intermediate-term bond funds.

Credit Quality

The second style component of bond funds measures the credit risk. For example, if your fund owns a bond from that car wash we talked about earlier in this chapter, credit risk measures the likelihood that the company will be able to pay off its loan to you. Credit-rating companies (Moody's Investors Service and Standard & Poor's) analyze companies' finances and come up with a final letter grade to measure their health. Each company has its own grading system. The best rating at Standard & Poor's is AAA; the worst is D. At Moody's the best is Aaa and the worst is C.

High-quality bond funds have average ratings of AA or higher, medium-quality funds have average ratings of BBB through A, and low-quality funds have average ratings below BB, according to Morningstar. Some fund managers are willing to take a risk on the lower-credit-quality, higher-risk bonds in hopes of winning higher yields. They are taking a chance on bonds from shaky companies that could potentially go bust.

Active versus Passive: To Index or Not to Index

The terms *active* and *passive* help define the way a fund is managed rather than what it manages. You can have small-cap, mid-cap, large-cap, value, growth, or blend funds, and each of these can be active or passive.

With active funds, an individual manager or management team selects specific stocks or bond investments to achieve a certain goal, like beating a benchmark. Examples are Fidelity Magellan, Janus Twenty, and T. Rowe Price Growth Stock. With passive funds, the management doesn't make its own investment choices but instead picks stocks to mirror a benchmark, like the S&P 500 or Russell 2000 index of small-cap stocks. Examples are the USAA S&P 500 Index or Vanguard Small-Cap Index fund, and of course, the well-known Vanguard 500 Index fund.

Because they take less work, index funds tend to have much lower expenses than active funds. You don't get the chance to beat the benchmark, or even match it with less risk. But besides expenses, you should not expect to underperform the benchmark either. People who buy active funds are paying extra for the chance either to beat a certain market index or achieve a specific goal, like getting exposure to energy companies with an energy sector fund or lowering one's risk with a conservative stock fund.

Financial writers tend to frame the active/passive debate as a right or wrong approach. I don't see it that way. My view is this: If you're hiring an advisor like a financial planner, or if you're putting a lot of your own research effort into your game plan, then at least some of your investments should be active funds. If instead you're doing it yourself and want to minimize the time and energy it takes to manage your game plan, go with passive funds.

Benefits of Active Funds

I believe actively managed funds offer some significant benefits. It's not just that you can get the chance to beat the market. It's that you can also pick funds that might beat or match the market while incurring *less risk* than you'd face in an index fund. In fact, some active funds don't even try to beat an index like the S&P 500. They simply try to earn returns that are better than cash, but with less risk than one would experience investing in the overall market.

A couple of examples of potentially lower-risk funds (based on statistical measures tracked by Morningstar) are the Delafield fund and the American Funds' Capital Income Builder. Capital Income Builder relies on a combination of stocks, bonds, and cash that lowers risk and keeps the standard deviation below that of the S&P 500. The Delafield fund focuses on finding values among various types of company stocks, and is willing to put a chunk of money into cash (of course, you need to remember that past performance doesn't guarantee future results). Cash and bonds are investments that the S&P index funds can't frolic in—they're fully invested in stocks. Table 4.4 shows how the returns on these funds compare with the broader market: not as good in the good years, but a lot better in the bad years.

Table 4.4   **A Little Less Risk, Thank You**

	1997	1998	1999	2000	2001	1-Year Return	5-Year Return	10-Year Return
Capital Income Builder	23.3%	11.8%	–2.8%	12.5%	4.7%	–0.06%	6.4%	10.3%
Delafield	19.7%	–11.5%	8.4%	14.0%	32.2%	–0.43%	6.0%	NA
Vanguard S&P 500	33.2%	28.6%	21.1%	–9.1%	–12.0%	–23.6%	0.45%	10.1%

Source: Morningstar. One-, five-, and ten-year returns are through July 31, 2002, unless not available (NA). Returns include dividends. All returns for multiyears are average annual performances.

Then, of course, there are the funds that shoot to outperform the benchmarks. What does outperform mean? These funds don't necessarily beat the benchmark every year. But they aim to over time—5, 10, 20 years. In fact, highly successful managers almost never outperform the benchmark 100 percent of the time, according to analyses cited by the money management firm Tweedy, Browne (an outfit that has outperformed long-term). Rather, in a study of exceptional long-term track records of managers who use a value approach (buying stocks with downtrodden prices) managers generally outperformed about 60 to 70 percent of the time. (Dates ranged between 1964 and 1994, depending on the length of existence of the fund.) The periods of outperformance compensated for the underperforming spurts.

All of which means that if you're willing to put some effort into finding a top manager, or if you're willing to hire someone who has the ability to do that for you—and you're willing to stay the course—you stand to earn significantly better returns with active management. Even if the differences year to year between active managers and an index seem small, they add up. Tweedy, Browne cites one study indicating that if you could earn just 1 percent better than the S&P 500 Index over a certain 30-year period, you'd have 33 percent more money at the end of that period.

It's for all of these reasons that I personally do not use indexing as my predominant strategy in picking funds. If only 5 percent of the managers are beating a given index, I want to find them. From 1995 through 1998, the S&P 500 was the leading index and few managers beat it. People said: "It's a no-brainer—just put it all in the Index 500 fund." It sounds like the same people who said in 1999, "Just put it all in tech—it's a no-brainer." Unfortunately, not using your brain can lead to mediocre performance and unnecessary losses. That is exactly what happened with the S&P 500 fund and with tech in 2000, 2001, and most of 2002.

My approach is that if I can get a client better returns than an index like the S&P with the same risk, or the same returns as an index with less risk, that's a worthwhile result. It takes some work finding those funds. And there are no guarantees. But I believe the effort is worthwhile. And with all the good information that's available on funds these days, you can find them, too. Again, more on how to select funds in Chapter 6.

Step 4, Get the Fund Fever: Summing Up

So now you know the basic benefits of funds. Now it's time to start building a portfolio.

Chapter 5

Step 5: Get an Offense and a Defense

At this point we've talked about the game plan mind-set, risk, goals, and using mutual funds. This chapter is about structuring a portfolio that suits you. A key goal of a good plan is to properly allocate your portfolio so you'll end up diversified.

Diversification is achieved by spreading your assets among different asset classes, fund styles, and fund managers. Doing so ensures that your portfolio isn't too dependent on any one investment. Diversification reduces the risk to your principal, and that's a key goal of any game plan.

I like to think of diversification in terms of offense and defense. In sports, a good coach knows it's not enough to have just a good offense or just a good defense. To win consistently, you need both. In football, soccer, basketball, handball, and other sports you score when you have the ball. When your opponent has the ball, you go on the defense to try to prevent the other side from scoring. Occasionally, the defense scores because they recover a fumble or intercept a pass.

The same principle applies with investing. You need investments with the potential to yield the return you seek, but you also need investments to protect you in tough markets.

We want an investment team with the strongest offense and defense possible. Ideally, your portfolio should look much like the legendary San

Francisco 49er football team, the first team in history to win five Super Bowls. The team's coaches were careful to bring together players who performed exceptionally well in their positions but who also were outstanding in their interaction with one another. Sure, there may have been a few stars like quarterback Joe Montana and wide receiver Jerry Rice, but they wouldn't have been heroes without the very capable players who backed them up. (Cowboy fans: I know your team did great too, just a little later.)

To follow that analogy, stocks are considered offensive because, while risky, they can offer unlimited upside. Bonds are considered defensive because they are a fixed-income investment with a company or government guarantee and a definite maturity period. While their market value may fluctuate during the holding period, they are considered more stable than stocks.

Then there's the special team idea. This relates to industries that at times outperform the overall market. In football a special team is used for various plays and strategies—for instance, a kicking team or a receiving team. In investing that could mean bringing in a manager who specializes in a sector like health care or technology.

In sum, every investor needs a good offense and a good defense. Occasionally a special team can give an added kick to a portfolio. Together, an offense and a defense provide diversification.

Diversification—the right offense/defense balance—is achieved through allocation. There are three levels to the allocation process. They are:

1. Allocating among stocks, bonds, and cash.
2. Allocating by fund style, such as dividing your money between large-cap blend and small-cap value funds.
3. Allocating by picking the actual mutual funds to match the styles.

The importance of a well-thought-out allocation plan was underscored by a study done by Gary Brinson, one of the world's most respected money managers. He analyzed several pension plans and determined that up to 90 percent of the portfolio's returns resulted from how they were allocated. I think there are also other important components that affect the outcome of a given portfolio. Skilled managers and their ability to navigate fickle markets also play a role in the success of an investing game plan.

But if I had to point to one main factor in the success of an individual's financial investments, it would be allocation. *Winning the Loser's Game*, investment guru Charles Ellis' landmark book, put it well. Ellis wrote that wisely formulated investment policy was the foundation for constructing and managing portfolios over time. And asset mix, he said, was the single most important dimension of investment policy.

In this chapter, I discuss asset mix and styles—allocation levels one and two. Chapter 6 discusses picking funds—allocation level three. And Chapter 7 brings it all together with examples.

Four Sample Portfolios

With few exceptions every investment portfolio for any investor of any age or income should have an offense and a defense. The question is one of proportion. How much offense? How much defense?

This chapter provides four basic model portfolios: conservative, moderate, aggressive, and the bunker. With conservative, the emphasis is on defense; with aggressive, on offense. Moderate falls nicely in the middle. The bunker stands apart from the other three portfolios. It is on the

---

Hayden Play:
Whatever your age, get an offense and a defense.

Age gets too much focus in most financial planning assessments. Just because you're young doesn't mean you should be ultra-aggressive and lose all of your money. You can never really make up for time. In fact, youth is when you should be growing your money, not losing it. It is the early money you invest that compounds and grows the most dramatically over time. At the other extreme, there is no set age at which you can't afford some upside risk. Any age can warrant an investing offense and an investing defense.

far defensive end of the risk spectrum and should be reserved for use in extreme bear markets, like that of 2000–2002.

The models are just that—models. They're meant as a starting point. If you are working with an advisor and/or are doing significant research yourself, you may well want to tweak these models to create a customized portfolio that fits your needs. Indeed, many readers are surely holding some "legacy" investments, and it's not always easy to convert one's present portfolio to match a model overnight. There are factors to consider like the tax implications of selling, as well as current market conditions and personal financial circumstances. These model portfolios are meant as a guide, not rigid rules.

The four portfolios are designed roughly to achieve the return-rate ranges we discussed when you developed your goals in Chapter 3. The conservative portfolio is designed to reap a 5 to 6 percent annual return, the moderate portfolio is expected to return 7 to 8 percent, while the aggressive portfolio is aimed at returning 9 percent a year or more on average. Depending on how much of a bear market you're dealing with, the bunker portfolio would return anywhere from 3 to 6 percent, overlapping somewhat with the conservative portfolio. (As I mentioned earlier, these return rates are guidelines based on historical patterns and future expectations. They are not predictions for actual annual return rates year in and year out. Nor can they be guaranteed. Actual returns might be higher in hypergrowth periods but lower in down markets.)

Many financial planning guides slice and dice portfolios into far more than four options. There's income, ultra-conservative, ultra-aggressive. But for all the micromanagement, I've found that the three basic portfolios—that is, the conservative, moderate, and aggressive—will service nearly all investors well. In fact, the moderate will take care of the lion's share, no matter what your age, circumstances, or income.

There is, of course, one exception. That's the bunker portfolio. Based on what happened in the bear market of 2000–2002, I felt many of my clients needed a fourth kind of portfolio. When the market gets really tough, the moderate portfolio can take on the feel of an ultra-aggressive allocation. The bunker portfolio keeps you a bit in the market while providing hefty cushion from knockout blows. This portfolio is for people that cannot or should not hang in there with a buy-and-hold philosophy. In an extreme up market, I still feel the aggressive portfolio is the most risk I like my clients to take.

Bear markets aside, most people belong in the moderate portfolio, some in conservative, and a select few in aggressive. I almost always start a new client out with a moderate-risk portfolio. It has been the right decision for at least 80 percent of my clients.

Why? Because it's very hard to judge up front how much risk someone can handle. If you go with the moderate portfolio and find you want less or more risk down the road, you can more easily adjust your portfolio's allocation strategy along the way if it is not on either extreme of the spectrum.

Only once have I been chastised by a client for not starting with an aggressive portfolio. That happened in the late 1990s when the bullish stock market seemed like a no-lose proposition. By the time the bears took over in 2000-2002, that same client wished she had gone with the original moderate portfolio. Trust me here. If there is any question about how much risk to take, always start out with a lower-risk portfolio.

To make this point more clear, let's look at two different allocation scenarios. Imagine you have $100,000 to invest. One portfolio is invested extremely aggressively—about 95 percent of the money is in equities. The other is diversified with 65 percent in equities and the remainder in fixed-income securities and cash. Now, I ask you, which of these portfolios would you have stuck with over the three-year period outlined in Table 5.1?

If you are like many of the people I've proposed this to, you would have run for the hills at some point in the second year if you were in the aggressive portfolio. That means you wouldn't have been in the investment in the third year to reach the winning $135,000. If you had been getting a steady 10 percent annual return in the moderate portfolio, however, you would have had $133,000 in your bank account. Sure, that's $2,000 less than if you white-knuckled it through the aggressive approach. But it's a heck of a lot more than you'd have had if you bailed out of the aggressive portfolio in midstream.

Table 5.1   Aggressive Growth versus Moderate Risk

	Aggressive	Moderate
Initial investment	$100,000	$100,000
Year 1	+80%	+10%
Year 2	−50%	+10%
Year 3	+50%	+10%
Final portfolio value	$135,000	$133,000

Note: The hypothetical investment results are for illustrative purposes only and should not be deemed a representation of past or future results. Actual investment results may be more or less than those shown. This does not represent any specific product or service.

It all comes down to the importance of understanding the distinction between intellectual and emotional risk, an element of the risk tolerance issue discussed in Chapter 2. Your intellectual tolerance level has to do with your mind and how your thought process responds to information. Your emotional tolerance level has to do with feelings and how your heart navigates a given situation.

Initially many clients tell me that they know they can handle a 20 percent drop in their portfolios. I respect their statement, but I don't always believe it. Why? Because they're considering the future intellectually. In most cases when folks say that, they have never experienced the emotion that can follow a dramatic plunge in an investment's value.

I have found that when intellect and emotions are in conflict with regard to money, the emotions generally rule. The great majority of people emotionally overreact to volatility, with negative consequences for their commitment to a consistent investment game plan. That is why I start 80 percent of my clients with a moderate portfolio.

If you feel you are among those select few who can stand the downs along with the ups, consider the aggressive portfolio. But realize that this means that while you might win big, you might lose big, too. All investors face the challenge of determining the level of risk they can handle and then picking the appropriate portfolio to reflect that level. Whatever your ultimate choice, your portfolio should be one with general outlines you can stick with. Rick Mears, the champion auto racer and four-time winner of the Indianapolis 500, put it well. To finish first, Mears said, you must first finish.

Static versus Active Asset Allocation

Many clients ask me: If I choose a certain portfolio, do I have to stick with it? My view: While you don't want to make willy-nilly changes, there should be room for flexibility. In the industry, this issue is framed as the debate between static asset allocation and active asset allocation.

Static allocation embraces the idea of assigning certain pots of money to stocks, bonds, and cash, and then sticking with those percentages. The approach is based on the assumption that future returns on stocks, bonds, and cash will be consistent with their behavior historically. The idea is that if you stick to your percentages and wait long enough, you'll get the outcome you seek. If you choose this route, you would still take into consideration your tolerance for risk and your goals before setting the specifications for the percentage allocations. But once you allocate a set percentage for each asset class (e.g., 50 percent stocks, 40 percent bonds, 10 percent cash), you more or less put your portfolio on automatic pilot. You buy and sell not to take advantage of the new opportunities, but to keep these set percentages in line.

The static approach can have significant upside. Historically, stock and bond returns have been proven to be stable and predictable over the long term. The problem is, achieving that stability can take a very, very long time—to the tune of 20 years or more. Also, there's no assurance that any investment will ever achieve that result. This waiting game also disregards the very human need for shorter-term gratification. A set allocation could perform very poorly under certain market conditions, even for as long as a few years. If you can't brace yourself through those periods and you shift gears, then you forgo the benefits of the approach by selling at a loss. During the growth years of the 1990s, particularly 1995 through 1999, many investors were leaving advisors that were stuck in their static allocation. The static allocation was preventing the investor from benefiting from the outsized gains the booming market was offering.

Roger Gibson, a money manager and fierce defender of static allocation, didn't advocate moving money from bonds even when the stock
market was going gangbusters in the late 1990s. While this frustrated
many people who wanted better returns, Gibson had the last word when
the market began tumbling. In fact, bonds outperformed stocks for at
least two and a half years starting in 2000, as measured by the Lehman
Brothers Aggregate Bond Index and the Standard & Poor's 500 Index.

On the upside or the down, few investors can wait around for the
static strategy to work. But if they do, historically it does work, at least
over the past quarter century. If you don't have the patience for it, and
many investors don't, you can end up worse off by trying it, bagging the
plan, and ending up with no strategy at all.

Active allocation is a much more dynamic and flexible approach
that responds to economic and market conditions. Rather than maintain
set allocation decisions made early on, this approach gives you the freedom to respond to market opportunities, at least with a small percentage
of your money.

In my opinion active allocation is more realistic and ultimately
more effective because it addresses both investors' long-term goals
and their short-term psychological needs. It also leaves you wiggle
room. So, for example, in an extreme down market like we had from
2000 to 2002, you can scale back your risk and take sanctuary in the
bunker portfolio.

The danger in this method is that you will yield too much to short-
term thinking. Taken to the extreme, an investor could use active allocation as an excuse for jumping in and out of the market altogether.
Market timing should not be confused with smart active allocation.
Overreacting in the short term can quickly defeat the effectiveness of a
long-term plan.

You can avoid the market-timing pitfall by sticking with your allocation for a great percentage of your portfolio and being more opportunistic on the fringes, mostly with "special teams" or sector investing, which
I discuss in greater detail later in this chapter. It is on those outer bound-
aries of your portfolio that you might use a fund that is riskier—say one

like CGM Capital Development. Its manager, Ken Heebner, is known for investing in only 25 to 30 stocks.

Active allocation, then, helps you stick with your game plan by building flexibility into it from the start. How to implement active allocation is something I tackle in Chapter 9, on checking your progress. I raise the point here to emphasize that portfolio planning is not a one-time decision. It's an ongoing process. While you don't want to make an exception the rule, tweaking your portfolio plan along the way is healthy.

How Much Stock Do I Need?

Now let's look at the four sample portfolios: conservative, moderate, aggressive, and bunker. Approach these as you would shop for a suit or a special dress. You might be a size 33, or an 8, and that's the size you buy. But then you may go to a tailor or seamstress to make your outfit just the right fit for you. The same goes for these models. The one you ultimately choose should serve as a baseline, which you can then tailor to fit your needs. Take a look at the pie charts in Figures 5.1 through 5.4 to start figuring out which allocation strategy will fit you.

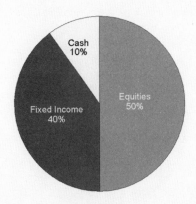

Figure 5.1   **Conservative Pie Chart**

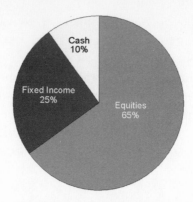

Figure 5.2   Moderate Pie Chart

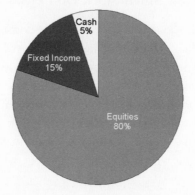

Figure 5.3   Aggressive Pie Chart

Figure 5.4   Bunker Pie Chart

Allocating: Stocks, Bonds, Cash

The Conservative Model

The portfolio shown in Table 5.2 is a low-risk portfolio and my second most conservative team. I have half of my resources allocated to offense and the other half to defense. You could think of the 10 percent in cash as a good player that I have sitting out the game on the sidelines. While it's on the bench, it's defensive. I will take that player off the bench if I see an opportunity to put him in the game, on either offense or another defensive play.

What kind of investor warrants such a portfolio? Someone who is risk averse, either psychologically or financially. This conservative portfolio suits a person who would choose a ride on a Ferris wheel over the heart-throbbing exhilaration of a world-class roller coaster. If you scored between 5 and 7 on the Risk Quiz in Chapter 2, then you might belong in this category.

In addition, anyone with shorter-term financial goals they want to achieve within four to five years should consider this conservative portfolio. Playing it safer makes it more likely that the money is available when it's needed. These goals might include buying a home or taking a sabbatical. When you get within two years of a goal, put all the money that you'll need for it in short-term bond funds or money market accounts. I would estimate the return on this kind of portfolio in the 5 to 6 percent range. But as the market environment changes, these returns will obviously fluctuate.

The Moderate Model

Compared with the conservative portfolio, the moderate portfolio (as shown in Table 5.3) steps up the octane by boosting the stock allocation

Table 5.2 **The Conservative Portfolio**

Equities	50%	(Offense)
Fixed income	40%	(Defense)
Cash	10%	(Defense)

Table 5.3   The Moderate Portfolio

Equities	65%	(Offense)
Fixed income	25%	(Defense)
Cash	10%	(Defense)

by 15 percentage points. This team's offense is stronger, which means we have a chance of scoring more in up markets but don't have as much protection in down markets. This portfolio is generally as aggressive as most people want to be.

Investors who think they should be more aggressive than this lineup may want to try this moderate allocation first. Still, don't let the moderate tag fool you. There is risk. During the bull market that predominated throughout much of the 1980s and 1990s, the moderate portfolio was the place to be. That changed after March 2000 when we started to move into a bear market. Since that time, this allocation probably hasn't done as well as the conservative portfolio, but generally I would expect returns of about 7 to 8 percent. Yet over the long term, I would still put the large majority of investors in a medium-risk portfolio similar to this one.

What kind of investor warrants this portfolio? A risk-steady person who can handle reasonable ups and downs of the market. This is a person who relishes the adrenaline rush of a good roller-coaster ride but would never consider skydiving. If you scored between 8 and 12 on the Risk Quiz, a moderate portfolio might be the category for you.

Good candidates for this portfolio have goals that are still five to seven years off. They can commit to giving the offense on this team time to work. They don't have to worry about needing to take the money out during a bear market like the early 2000s. This allocation could work for those seeking to fund a college education as well as for retirement goals.

The Aggressive Model

The aggressive allocation shown in Table 5.4 is only for the most optimistic, steel-nerved, and otherwise financially stable investor. Almost

Table 5.4 **The Aggressive Portfolio**

Equities	80%	(Offense)
Fixed income	15%	(Defense)
Cash	5%	(Defense)

every economic indicator in corporate America needs to look good to warrant this kind of aggressive portfolio. If earnings are falling, stock prices are fluctuating, and unemployment rates are climbing, you should reconsider whether the possibility of better returns is worth the risk of big losses.

For an aggressive scenario to succeed, you have to have an offense with funds that perform like a Michael Jordan in basketball or the Williams sisters in tennis. All economic environments do not offer such opportunities. I don't mean to scare you away from an aggressive portfolio entirely. Indeed, if you really have staying power—and don't overestimate the likelihood that you do—this portfolio is the place to be. This allocation gave the best returns from 1982 through early March of 2000.

But most folks understandably don't have the staying power to endure the grim downturns an allocation like this can encounter. Ultimately, this approach is for the type of investor who considers rollercoaster rides to be a normal way of life. Consider it if you scored 13 to 15 on the Risk Test and then only if you have at least several decades of income-earning years ahead and a high income that will give you a cushion should the worst happen.

The expected returns on this portfolio would be 9 percent or more over a long period of time. That may sound sweet compared with the other two portfolios. But remember it comes with high volatility—harsh down years amid the good that can erase the gains of those years.

If you do go with this portfolio, active asset allocation can be key in offsetting risk. When you see whopping gains in a particular investment—say 40, 50 percent or more in a sector fund—it is time to take some gains and recalibrate the portfolio. It takes discipline, but it helps avoid the downsides that this portfolio has in store. More on how to manage such tweaks in Chapter 9.

Choose aggressive only if you have seven years or more to wait for the results, as it can take that long to overcome a down market cycle with this portfolio. (And again, nothing is guaranteed.) If you lose big on the way to winning big it will take significant time to recover. Table 5.5 shows just how much it can take to get back to even and gives new meaning to the old saying, "You win by not losing."

One final warning note on the aggressive portfolio: Whatever you do, don't try to overcome past extraordinary losses with an aggressive portfolio. The market isn't that generous. If you've lost a lot of money, the best solution is to regroup as though you were starting fresh. If that means a more conservative portfolio, that would be the right approach, even if you had suffered severe losses previously.

The Bunker Model

Finally, when all else seems to be failing (and the market is tumbling), there's the bunker portfolio (see Table 5.6). It should be considered somewhat apart from the other three. I see it as a kind of stopgap measure for bear markets. It's designed to ensure you have money left once

Table 5.5   **The Long Road to Recovery**

If an Investment Loses This Much . . .	. . . It Must Earn This Just to Recover Losses
10%	11%
20%	25%
30%	43%
40%	67%
50%	100%
60%	150%
70%	233%
80%	400%
90%	900%

Table 5.6 The Bunker Portfolio

Equities	30%	(Offense)
Fixed income	55%	(Defense)
Cash	15%	(Defense)

the market finally turns around. It does not eliminate risk though it helps lower it. In an up market I wouldn't recommend it. If you need your money for a short-term goal in a year or two, don't play around even with this. You should simply be out of the market.

I've named it the bunker because sometimes the most you can hope for is shelter from the market's storm. I named it after the huge cement one-story buildings that I used to retreat to during the severe weather that often buffeted northern Greenland when I was serving in the Air Force back in 1965. Despite winds that gusted to over 100 miles per hour, we all knew we could survive if we could just make it to the safety of the buildings. They were built like the Rock of Gibraltar.

The stock market equivalent of those storms is the Great Bear Market that started in March 2000. I relied on portfolios similar to this bunker model to help my clients make it through that and other prolonged bear markets. Technically this portfolio has the most defense of all four portfolios. But in a bear market you may actually find that the fixed income, typically considered defense, is the component that's giving you the positive returns. Likewise, your stock funds may be playing a defensive role in your portfolio. They're there to protect you so that you are ready when the market turns around.

So there you have it. Those are the four models. Table 5.7 is designed to help you figure out which portfolio type might be appropriate given your financial goals and risk tolerance. Now we'll go on to analyzing the detailed fund styles that will comprise each asset category of your portfolio.

Table 5.7   Finding a Portfolio That Suits You

	Bunker	*Conservative*	*Moderate*	*Aggressive*
Investor Profile				
Risk Quiz score	5 to 7	5 to 7	8 to 12	13 to 15
Your driving style	Obey speed limit	Obey speed limit	Sometimes drive 10 mph over speed limit	Sometimes drive 15 mph over speed limit
Preferred sport	Most sports, but defensive plays	Gardening/ golf	Tennis/ football	Rugby/ skydiving
Goals	Protecting principal	Shorter-term	Mid-term	Long-term
Goal examples	Home, car, retirement	Home, car, retirement	College/ retirement	Retirement
Time needed	4 to 5 Years	4 to 5 Years	5 to 7 years	7 years or more
Investment Profile				
Risk of losses	Low	Low	Medium	High
Relative returns	3% to 6%	5% to 6%	7% to 8%	9% plus

Making Sense of the Style Game

After selecting a model portfolio, it's time to move to the second level of allocation. Here's where we populate that portfolio with a healthy selection of varied fund styles, the kind discussed in Chapter 4 (e.g., value, growth, large-cap, small-cap). The pie charts in Figures 5.5 through 5.8 illustrate how this is done.

Allocating: Fund Styles

Selecting the appropriate fund to fit your choice of style can seem like tricky business, because managers and analysts interpret the style and size

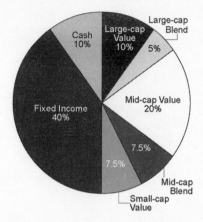

Figure 5.5   Conservative Pie Chart

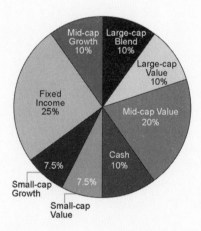

Figure 5.6   Moderate Pie Chart

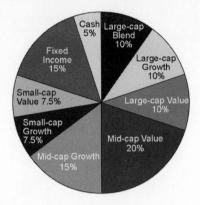

Figure 5.7   Aggressive Pie Chart

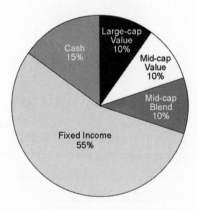

Figure 5.8   Bunker Pie Chart

labels differently. Let's take the value style as an example. So-called deep or extreme value managers are strictly disciplined in the Benjamin Graham–Warren Buffett tradition. They look for strong companies whose stocks they believe are deeply discounted from their intrinsic value and buy only if they can find a bargain. If the stock price eventually rises as they expect, they sell when they believe it has reached its true value, even if they suspect that investor psychology might push the stock price up further. They typically sell before the company in question is considered a growth stock.

A second type of value manager is less rigid. He or she might buy a stock that isn't dirt cheap, but seems priced at a small discount to its worth (as measured by assets, earnings, or other indicia). If a value stock's price rises enough to reflect the true worth of the company and continues upward, this type of manager might still hold that stock even after it could reasonably be reclassified as a growth play. The less rigid a value manager is about price concerns, the more he or she starts to blend in with the growth style—thus, the Morningstar style label "blend." If you've heard the phrase "growth at a reasonable price" (GARP), it's for managers who are trying to achieve the best of both worlds—some growth potential in a stock without paying too high a price.

The difference between one value manager and the next can result in a substantial variation in returns. Consider Bob Sanborn, a deep value fund manager who built a great track record at the Oakmark Fund until 1998. That's when Sanborn's fund was up only 3.7 percent, underperforming the S&P 500 by about 25 percentage points. In 1999 Sanborn's fund lost 10.5 percent, underperforming the S&P 500 by about 32 percentage points.

At a certain point Sanborn's commitment to deep value investing—and a resulting two-year whacking—became too much. Sanborn stepped down from the fund. He was replaced by Bill Nygren, a value manager who manages the Oakmark Select Fund. Nygren had very acceptable returns in 1998 and 1999 in his Select Fund despite his value orientation. Nygren was more flexible in his interpretation of value.

He was picking stocks that weren't so deeply discounted as those that Bob was buying.

Varying degrees of style span the stock fund category. As an investor, you'll want to do some research to make sure you have a firm grasp on where your funds fit on the spectrum. Unfortunately, the process of determining this is sometimes more an art than a science. Formal quantitative data don't always reflect style subtleties. But this is where you'll need to stay informed and gain more insight by keeping up with returns and the reliable mutual fund commentators and analysts. It's at this point that many people seek an advisor or a Certified Financial Planner to help them put their game plans together. Let's look at how each of the four sample portfolios could be allocated on the style level.

The Conservative Portfolio

As shown in Table 5.8, this conservative portfolio is designed to protect your money in a down market (but not necessarily a prolonged bear market). The majority of the stock investments are in value funds, but I've diversified the portfolio somewhat by spreading the value out across funds that invest in a range of different-sized companies. The largest stock allocations are to large-cap value and mid-cap value. You'll also notice there are no pure growth styles in this portfolio. We try to pick up some growth through the blend funds, which provide a more hedged approach to higher-return opportunities. Now let's look at the fixed-income part of the portfolio (see Table 5.9).

Table 5.8 **Conservative Portfolio Stock Fund Style Mix**

	Value	Blend	Growth	Total
Large-cap	10%	5%	0%	15%
Medium-cap	20%	7.5%	0%	27.5%
Small-cap	7.5%	0%	0%	7.5%
Total	37.5%	12.5%	0%	50%

Table 5.9   Conservative Portfolio Bond Fund Style Mix

	Short-Term	Intermediate-Term	Long-Term	Total
High-quality	20%	20%	0%	40%
Medium-quality	0%	0%	0%	0%
Low-quality	0%	0%	0%	0%
Total	20%	20%	0%	40%

We've invested 40 percent of the money in our portfolio into bonds because we want the steady defensive play of fixed income. This example assumes that interest rates are either at or near historic lows, as they were in 2001 and 2002. In such an environment, our chief concern is rising interest rates that drive down bond values. So we are going to avoid all long-term bonds in all four portfolios, because if rates start rising the value on those bonds is likely to fall more sharply than on short- and intermediate-term bonds. We are also going to stay with bond funds that invest in high-quality investment-rated bonds because the companies behind the bonds are less likely to default. That lowers the risk, which is the goal with this portfolio.

The 10 percent in cash will be put into a money market fund that pays a competitive interest rate. This money may be deployed whenever we think there is opportunity in the market.

The Moderate Portfolio

The moderate portfolio shown in Table 5.10 not only has more of its money invested in stocks than the conservative portfolio, but it has 17.5 percent of

Table 5.10   Moderate Portfolio Stock Fund Style Mix

	Value	Blend	Growth	Total
Large-cap	10%	10%	0%	20%
Medium-cap	20%	0%	10%	30%
Small-cap	7.5%	0%	7.5%	15%
Total	37.5%	10%	17.5%	65%

that money invested in growth funds. This tact ratchets up the opportunity to secure higher returns as well as the risk of greater losses. But we still aim to take only moderate risk. The growth funds could take a significant hit in down market years but could lead to a rebound in the better years.

As with the conservative portfolio, the moderate portfolio's bond fund mix guards against the threat of rising interest rates (see Table 5.11). While we've got comparatively less money invested in bonds, we are still playing it safe by sticking with high-quality short- and intermediate-term funds. Again, as with the conservative portfolio, the cash that comprises the remaining 10 percent of the portfolio's value would be invested in a money market fund.

Aggressive Portfolio

The aggressive portfolio, shown in Table 5.12, is the highest-risk portfolio of the three. The real potential for danger in this portfolio is the tendency of investors to pick highly focused funds—those with no more than 30 stocks—or sector funds, which represent only a narrow industry like energy or tech.

Table 5.11   **Moderate Portfolio Bond Fund Style Mix**

	Short-Term	Intermediate-Term	Long-Term	Total
High-quality	10%	15%	0%	25%
Medium-quality	0%	0%	0%	0%
Low-quality	0%	0%	0%	0%
Total	10%	15%	0%	25%

Table 5.12   **Aggressive Portfolio Stock Fund Style Mix**

	Value	Blend	Growth	Total
Large-cap	10%	10%	10%	30%
Medium-cap	20%	0%	15%	35%
Small-cap	7.5%	0%	7.5%	15%
Total	37.5%	10%	32.5%	80%

To avoid the problems that this kind of investment concentration can cause, the great majority of the 80 percent of this portfolio that is in stock mutual funds should be almost evenly diversified between growth and value. In addition, most of those funds should offer another level of diversification: Choose only funds that are allocating your money in at least four industries or sectors.

As shown in Table 5.13, this portfolio allocates two-thirds of its bond component to intermediate-term bonds, which generally offer slightly higher interest than short-term bonds in exchange for additional risk if interest rates go up. Still, I've remained with the relative safety of high-quality bond funds; the managers can make adjustments as interest rates rise. Think of the fixed-income element of the aggressive portfolio as the place to carve out some security for yourself—even in a relatively charged portfolio.

The Bunker Portfolio

As shown in Table 5.14, the bunker portfolio is not a place for risk taking. That's why the equities component has been scaled back—

Table 5.13 **Aggressive Portfolio Bond Fund Style Mix**

	Short-Term	Intermediate-Term	Long-Term	Total
High-quality	5%	10%	0%	15%
Medium-quality	0%	0%	0%	0%
Low-quality	0%	0%	0%	0%
Total	5%	10%	0%	15%

Table 5.14 **Bunker Portfolio Stock Fund Style Mix**

	Value	Blend	Growth	Total
Large-cap	10%	0%	0%	10%
Medium-cap	10%	10%	0%	20%
Small-cap	0%	0%	0%	0%
Total	20%	10%	0%	30%

even in comparison to the conservative portfolio. With the stock funds that you are allocating, you want to stick mostly with value funds. Those are usually the best ones to retreat to in a down market. But I've also put 10 percent in blend. That's a kind of low-risk hedge. It gives you a chance at catching some upside improvement when the markets turn around.

The bear market can be a time for bonds to shine. Because of this, the bunker portfolio loads up with them (see Table 5.15). The sizable bond component plays two roles. It reduces risk by avoiding the volatility of stocks at the same time that it offers you some opportunity for going on the offensive and making a play based on interest rates.

The important thing to remember here is to stick with high-quality bond funds. Remember, down markets are just that—downers. Bankruptcy lawyers aside, it's usually not an easy time for any sector of the economy. In the end, you need the company or entity that issues your funds' bonds to stay afloat if you hope to make any money. High-quality bond funds help ensure this. And finally, because nothing is certain in these markets, I raise the cash level to 15 percent.

Special Teams

Now that you have an idea of what kind of offense and defense you want to build for yourself, we need to review one secret weapon: special teams. In football, special teams are players brought into the game to achieve very specific plays, such as kicking a field goal or receiving the football

Table 5.15   Bunker Portfolio Bond Fund Style Mix

	Short-Term	Intermediate-Term	Long-Term	Total
High-quality	27.5%	27.5%	0%	55%
Medium-quality	0%	0%	0%	0%
Low-quality	0%	0%	0%	0%
Total	27.5%	27.5%	0%	55%

on a kickoff. But generally that is their special role on the team and they do little more.

In investing, the analogy to special teams is sector funds, funds that invest in a specific industry or type of stock, like energy or real estate stocks, health care, or even a narrow region like Korea. Sector funds are used mostly to add a little extra return to a portfolio. Of course, that generally means adding risk. On the risk scale of 1 to 10 (10 being highest), sectors would be 8 to 10.

Playing with sectors is like playing with matches when you were a kid. When you light up a match, you can get burned if you hold it for too long. The same goes for sectors. Even seemingly invincible industries, like tech of the late 1990s, can lose money faster than ice melting on a hot stove. To succeed with sectors you need to have the knack for knowing when to buy in, and when to sell. Yes, folks, it's market timing. But here you're faced with that age-old challenge of buying low and selling high; most investors buy high and sell low particularly in volatile sectors. That's why I advocate sector investing for only a small portion of your portfolio.

For the bulk of your portfolio, you're almost always better off with a strong diversified manager who buys stocks across sectors for the long term. But just as we learn to use matches, judicious use of sectors can be advantageous.

The benefits of sector investing are twofold. First, a smart sector bet can reap great rewards. Take gold (not an official industry sector but an investing subspecialty nonetheless). Gold funds were up on average more

---

Hayden Play:
Avoid sectors unless you can handle the high-risk adrenaline rushes.

Industry sectors are sexy but dangerous, as they cycle in and out of favor so fast. Those tempted should keep their sector investments to small doses, pay close attention, and act quickly. If you want more excitement, I recommend Vegas.

than 64 percent for the first five and a half months of 2002, compared with a 13 percent loss for the S&P 500 funds that track the broader market over the same time period. But if you didn't sell you could have lost very quickly, as the *Investor's Business Daily* Gold Index dropped over 30 percent in one week toward the end of July 2002. Too bad for the people who had just decided to chase it.

The second potential advantage of sector investing is the possibility of psychological satisfaction. If most of your portfolio is diversified among hundreds of stocks through broadly invested mutual funds, your returns at any given moment may be solid but they'll rarely be stellar. The downside of diversified investing is that by limiting your risk you may also limit your return in the short run. With sector investing, you can satiate your craving to be where the action is and go for a big hit. By limiting your roll of the dice to a small portion of your portfolio (and it is gambling—don't kid yourself otherwise!) you get that psychological kick and potential financial reward without overexposing yourself to too much loss. Your rule of thumb for sector investing should be to only invest what you can afford to lose and even then do so very, very carefully.

Making a call on a sector fund takes research, common sense, and intuition. The research can come from books, magazines, newsletters, newspapers, the Internet, and fund managers. I personally try to recognize a trend and move into it when it seems obvious and out of it at the first real sign of deterioration. Getting out is the key. As the tech debacle exemplifies, the biggest mistake most folks make with sector investing is staying in too long.

There's no requirement to invest in sectors. No matter how aggressive your inclinations, if you want to stick with diversified funds you'll do just fine. No pressure. In fact, most people lose money because they tend to chase high-return hot sectors just before the inevitable drop in the market, like that precipitous drop in gold. So if you're still interested in sectors, I bet you're wondering how much is enough. Generally I would not invest more than 10 percent of a portfolio in sectors. Three to five percent is an even better range.

Step 5, Get an Offense and a Defense: Summing Up

By now, you should have an idea of how to allocate your investment funds. First, to the asset classes of stocks, bonds, and cash, and second, to the styles of investments within those classes. Each portfolio provides a game plan with varying degrees of offense and defense. The conservative portfolio is very defensive with mostly bonds and value funds. The moderate portfolio is fairly evenly weighted but overall has a stronger offense than defense. The aggressive portfolio, which I don't recommend to many people, is mostly offense and has a limited defense. Finally, think of the bunker portfolio as your ultimate defense. It's your star goalie, skilled at protecting your principal from the ravages of the market's bears.

The allocations in these sample portfolios should be adjusted at the outset to fit your individual situation. Those factors can include anything from your work or financial circumstances to the simple realities of contending with what you already own. Sometimes it's not so easy to—*poof*—change a constellation of funds that you're currently holding to match another pie chart entirely. That's okay. The key is to make sure you've got an offense and a defense that to some degree suit your circumstances.

Now let's move on to Chapter 6, where we'll discuss how to pick the best managers and funds to fit your portfolio.

Chapter 6

Step 6: Pick the Players

Consider the high school soccer coach who attends a two-week summer camp to learn about the latest strategies for building a good team. Now it's fall and tryout week is underway. If she doesn't choose the right players for the appropriate positions, all her off-season work will be for nothing. For her team to succeed, the coach must put her newfound knowledge into action.

The same goes for you, the investor, as you prepare to pick specific funds for your portfolio. So far you've decided on the general portfolio and allocation that you want to pursue. You've further refined your allocation by deciding which styles of funds to seek out. Now you need to select the best and the brightest to execute your game plan strategy.

On both offense and defense, you want the very best players in the leagues to fill those allocation slots.

Ultimately, fund selection is where the rubber of all the investing theory meets the often bumpy road of market reality. I particularly relish this part of the game plan, and I hope you will, too. While your overall allocation will greatly determine the success of your game plan, the more successful managers can enhance that return through superior performance. Just as there are superior players for a team, there are also superior managers. Finding those is our goal at this level of allocation.

Deciding which funds deserve your hard-earned money is an important task. Just any fund won't do—even if it is in the exact style and asset category you want. Just as all good soccer goalies differ from one another, funds within a given style type each offer varying degrees of potential for risks and rewards.

When assessing a fund, it's very important that it be in line with your overall portfolio allocation that we discussed in Chapter 5—and that it's meeting your goals at the same time that it fits your ability to handle risk.

You should be able to find appropriate funds for your portfolio needs from the thousands of funds on the market. How do you distinguish between apparently similar-style funds? Some of the criteria used to judge funds can get very technical very quickly. But when it is broken down, nearly all the important information can be traced back to some basic who, what, where, and how questions.

Finding Funds to Make the Cut

- **What** style funds do you need to fit your allocation strategy?
- **How** many funds are enough?
- **What** is the fund's track record? Look closely at 1987, 1990, 1994, 2000, 2001, and 2002. What was the fund's performance when the markets stumbled?
- **Who** manages the fund, how experienced is he or she, and how consistent has he or she been?
- **How** much will it cost, and how much risk will it entail?
- **Where** (stocks/bonds/industries) does the fund invest your money?

Each of these questions will lead you to other criteria you might want to consider about each fund. Over time, either investors develop their own systems, their own artful approaches to the science of investing, or they work with advisors. I'll walk you through the process that I use to screen funds and outline the criteria that make or break my fund picks. But you'll soon develop your own system and those research techniques, and your fund needs will evolve over time. No one fund is right for all investors or all portfolios all the time.

How Many Funds Are Enough?

Before starting your fund selection, it's good to have a general idea of how many you are looking for. This depends a good deal on the amount of money you want to invest, what your objectives are, and how much risk you want to take. Also, always remember that the funds must match your overall allocation.

One reason people have several funds is because they may want to go beyond their core holdings and invest in specific sector funds. By doing so they should know they substantially increase risk in their portfolios, as we discussed in Chapter 5.

You also need to be careful not to spread yourself too thin. Some funds have minimum investment amounts of anywhere from $1,000 to $10,000. Sometimes it's even higher. If you have limited money to invest, there are only so many funds you can buy shares in.

Table 6.1 should be used only as a general guideline. It assumes you are not using any sector funds. If you use any special team/sector funds you would need to add one or two sector funds per portfolio, but generally, as I've said before, you should limit them to no more than 10 percent of your portfolio. Of course, the chart also assumes you have already allocated specific percentages of your portfolio to offense and defense.

You'll also probably notice that investing under $100,000 into seven or fewer funds may not enable you to meet all the percentage al-

Table 6.1 **How Many Is Enough?**

Investment Size	Number of Funds (Not Including Special Team/ Sector Funds)
Up to $50,000	4 to 5 funds
$50,000 to $100,000	6 to 7 funds
$100,000 to $500,000	8 to 10 funds
$500,000 and more	11 to 15 funds

locations of the model portfolios in Chapter 5. Don't sweat it. As I've said, you'll simply want to use the portfolios as guidelines. As you have more money to invest, you'll be able to choose more funds that will further diversify your portfolio. Alternately, if you have an advisor, you and your advisor can create your own allocation formula for any amount you have.

What Is the Fund's Track Record?

Avoiding the Top 10 Trap

Many of my clients walk into my office with a newspaper or magazine article ranking last year's hottest funds. Their question: Why not just pick the most profitable funds from last year and let it rip? My answer: It just doesn't work that way. If I had my way, I'd eliminate all such ranking charts because I think they wrongly focus investors on a fund's short-term history rather than the long-term track record.

Pulling Rank:
The Numbers behind the Numbers

When comparing funds by rankings, it is important to understand the difference between a percentage ranking and a numerical ranking. In Table 6.2 you will notice columns showing the percentage rank as compared with the fund's category. A fund in the top 1 percent shares its spotlight with others. By that I mean that if there are 3,000 funds in the category and a fund has a 1 percent ranking, it is just one of 30 funds rated in the top 1 percent (3,000 × .01 = 30). While the top 25 funds are ranked by percentage in each year, they are ranked numerically for the entire period of 11 years to actually show the top 25 funds over the long term. Separately, Table 6.3 shows an actual numerical ranking of performance to reveal the 10 top-performing funds for each year. When funds are ranked numerically as they are in the latter chart, they stand alone in all their statistical glory.

Paradoxically, to help you better understand the danger of focusing exclusively on this type of ranking, I'd like to compare two ranking charts chock-full of data. The King of the World chart (Table 6.2) ranks the top 25 U.S. diversified and world stock funds by their average annual returns over an 11-year period from 1991 through December 2001. The King for a Year chart (Table 6.3) ranks the top 10 funds for each year over the same 11 years.

I think the secrets of a successful long-term game plan are embedded within these tables. They drive home a central point that can't be repeated enough in investing: Don't be swayed by recent success stories of what could be one-trick ponies. Instead, find consistent players that have proven their merit over time. Investors who win the game are those with an awareness of the cycles of the market and the risks it entails. They are committed to investing in a diversified game plan by putting their money with consistent managers.

So let's go to the charts. The King of the World chart shows that over the 11-year period, FPA Capital returned an impressive average annual return of 21.9 percent, making it the best-performing fund in Morningstar's U.S. diversified stock and world stock fund category from 1991 through 2001. Yet in the King for a Year table you can see that FPA only made it into the top 10 ranking in one year—2001.

At this point you might be wondering why am I so impressed by FPA if it's not a consistent enough performer to stay in the top 10 ranking. Why? Because that kind of one-time outsized performance doesn't matter to me—nor is it very realistic. Very few funds remain in the top 10 list year in and year out. So what kind of consistency should you look for?

I want a manager, in this case FPA Capital's Bob Rodriguez, who invests money in a manner that's consistent with his investment philosophy. As you will see in the brief profile on Bob in Chapter 8, he is a deep value contrarian. At times he will buy stocks that nobody, certainly not the traditional Wall Street boys and girls, would touch. He is highly disciplined, so when his method of picking stocks is out of favor

Table 6.2 King of the World: The Top 25 U.S. Diversified and World Stock Funds by Average Annual Return over 11 Years through December 31, 2001

Fund Name	Category	Average Annual Return over 11 Years	1991 Return	1991 % Rank	1992 Return	1992 % Rank	1993 Return	1993 % Rank	1994 Return	1994 % Rank	1995 Return	1995 % Rank
1. FPA Capital	Small Value	21.87%	64.51%	1	21.57%	35	16.74%	58	10.37%	1	38.39%	4
2. Calamos Growth A	Mid-cap Growth	21.03	40.21	74	1.71	81	4.35	92	-5.70	82	27.50	79
3. INVESCO Leisure Inv	Mid-cap Growth	20.80	52.71	12	23.41	13	35.71	1	-4.98	76	15.79	99
4. Smith Barney Aggressive Growth A	Large Growth	20.51	42.67	47	2.03	83	21.10	11	-1.65	47	35.75	26
5. Merrill Lynch Small Cap Value A	Small Blend	20.48	54.87	8	17.04	41	14.26	62	3.81	18	22.34	65
6. Fidelity Low-Priced Stock	Small Value	20.23	46.26	25	28.95	14	20.21	32	4.81	10	24.89	44
7. Wasatch Core Growth	Small Growth	20.15	40.80	52	4.72	90	11.12	80	2.68	29	40.42	9
8. Wasatch Small Cap Growth	Small Growth	20.00	50.42	57	4.73	81	22.49	27	5.50	17	28.12	68
9. Federated Kaufmann K	Mid-cap Growth	19.77	79.43	4	11.32	32	18.18	34	8.99	8	36.89	35
10. Heartland Value	Small Value	19.76	49.35	8	42.48	1	18.77	47	1.71	28	29.80	19
11. Weitz Partners Value	Mid-cap Value	19.73	28.00	52	15.14	43	23.03	25	-8.97	85	38.66	10
12. Berger Small Cap Value Instl	Small Value	19.63	24.86	83	19.72	50	16.09	64	6.70	4	26.09	39

#	Fund	Category										
13.	Hartford Capital Appreciation HLS 1A	Large Blend	19.61	54.13	4	16.73	24	20.93	21	2.56	10	30.27	45
14.	Legg Mason Value Prim	Large Blend	19.58	34.73	16	11.44	33	11.26	70	1.39	24	40.76	5
15.	UAM ICM Small Company	Small Value	19.45	48.67	12	32.28	7	22.03	20	3.41	21	21.27	68
16.	Spectra N	Large Growth	19.40	57.35	23	8.37	30	27.67	2	3.65	9	47.71	3
17.	Mairs & Power Growth	Large Blend	19.35	42.09	10	7.87	41	12.83	30	5.66	4	47.70	1
18.	Merrill Lynch Small Cap Value B	Small Blend	19.26	53.32	13	15.84	45	13.07	72	2.79	27	21.12	71
19.	Pimco Renaissance C	Mid-cap Value	19.23	33.24	43	7.78	86	21.23	41	-5.05	73	27.61	54
20.	Strong Advisor Common Stock Z	Mid-cap Blend	19.17	65.68	2	20.78	19	25.38	20	-0.49	45	32.41	31
21.	Van Kampen Emerging Growth A	Large Growth	19.16	60.43	19	9.73	24	23.92	6	-7.13	88	44.63	7
22.	Longleaf Partners	Mid-cap Value	19.14	39.17	18	20.50	21	22.23	37	8.97	4	27.48	57
23.	Liberty Acorn Z	Small Growth	19.12	47.41	74	24.23	6	32.35	4	-7.45	86	20.80	85
24.	Delaware Trend A	Mid-cap Growth	19.11	74.49	8	22.40	3	22.37	20	-9.97	96	42.51	18
25.	Oppenheimer Main St Growth & Income A	Large Blend	18.93	66.37	1	31.80	1	35.39	1	-1.53	65	30.77	71

Source: Morningstar, Inc. Although data are gathered from reliable sources, Morningstar cannot guarantee completeness and accuracy. Percentage rankings are versus funds' own categories for the year.

Table 6.2 *(Continued)*

Fund Name	Category	1996 Return	1996 % Rank	1997 Return	1997 % Rank	1998 Return	1998 % Rank	1999 Return	1999 % Rank	2000 Return	2000 % Rank	2001 Return	2001 % Rank
1. FPA Capital	Small Value	37.76%	8	17.70%	98	-0.42%	17	14.24%	20	-3.08%	97	38.13%	3
2. Calamos Growth A	Mid-cap Growth	37.91	2	25.18	22	27.31	18	77.70	30	26.59	5	-7.68	15
3. INVESCO Leisure Inv	Mid-cap Growth	9.08	94	26.46	19	29.78	14	65.59	38	-7.97	55	4.10	3
4. Smith Barney Aggressive Growth A	Large Growth	2.73	99	28.58	38	35.05	39	63.74	12	19.25	1	-5.00	2
5. Merrill Lynch Small Cap Value A	Small Blend	23.90	32	25.23	43	-5.58	50	33.32	14	15.70	29	30.64	4
6. Fidelity Low–Priced Stock	Small Value	26.89	26	26.73	74	0.53	16	5.08	42	18.83	54	26.71	12
7. Wasatch Core Growth	Small Growth	16.54	75	27.55	20	1.56	56	19.35	79	37.39	1	28.82	1
8. Wasatch Small Cap Growth	Small Growth	5.20	94	19.23	48	11.17	22	40.87	61	16.80	10	24.17	3
9. Federated Kaufmann K	Mid-cap Growth	20.92	28	12.56	79	0.72	88	26.01	82	10.86	18	7.85	2
10. Heartland Value	Small Value	20.99	67	23.19	86	-11.46	76	25.01	11	2.03	91	29.45	8
11. Weitz Partners Value	Mid-cap Value	19.04	61	40.64	1	29.13	1	22.02	9	21.08	39	-0.86	77
12. Berger Small Cap Value Instl	Small Value	25.60	33	36.93	21	1.83	13	14.69	19	27.16	19	20.42	29

#	Fund	Category												
13.	Hartford Capital Appreciation HLS IA	Large Blend	20.56	47	22.49	82	15.50	78	37.52	6	13.15	4	-7.09	12
14.	Legg Mason Value Prim	Large Blend	38.43	2	37.05	2	48.04	1	26.71	19	-7.14	47	-9.29	19
15.	UAM ICM Small Company	Small Value	23.01	45	33.01	40	-0.51	18	-1.07	65	22.46	36	19.05	34
16.	Spectra N	Large Growth	19.38	44	24.62	58	47.96	11	72.01	8	-32.45	98	-17.49	29
17.	Mairs & Power Growth	Large Blend	27.76	7	28.67	49	9.36	92	7.17	92	26.47	1	6.48	2
18.	Merrill Lynch Small Cap Value B	Small Blend	22.57	43	23.97	53	-6.55	61	31.93	16	14.55	33	29.33	6
19.	Pimco Renaissance C	Mid-cap Value	24.40	21	34.90	9	10.72	17	9.02	46	36.66	8	18.51	11
20.	Strong Advisor Common Stock Z	Mid-cap Blend	20.47	46	19.13	81	6.42	48	40.35	7	-1.20	68	-1.70	46
21.	Van Kampen Emerging Growth A	Large Growth	17.91	53	21.34	76	34.73	41	103.72	2	-11.36	36	-32.59	88
22.	Longleaf Partners	Mid-cap Value	21.02	42	28.25	31	14.28	7	2.19	61	20.60	40	10.35	36
23.	Liberty Acorn Z	Small Growth	22.55	32	24.98	28	6.02	35	33.38	67	10.06	19	6.14	16
24.	Delaware Trend A	Mid-cap Growth	10.71	81	19.43	46	13.57	58	71.33	34	-6.79	51	-14.88	31
25.	Oppenheimer Main St	Large Blend	15.70	89	26.59	59	25.19	42	17.12	69	-7.94	51	-10.46	26

Source: Morningstar, Inc. Although data are gathered from reliable sources, Morningstar cannot guarantee completeness and accuracy. Percentage rankings are versus funds' own categories for the year.

Table 6.3   King for a Year: The Top 10 Funds for 11 Years

Year	Dominant Style	Fund Name	Category	Return
1991	**Growth**			
		1 CGM Capital Development	Mid-cap Value	99.08%
		2 Montgomery Small Cap R	Small-cap Growth	98.75
		3 American Heritage	World Stock	96.59
		4 Berger Growth	Large-cap Growth	88.81
		5 Waddell & Reed Adv New Concepts A	Mid-cap Growth	88.09
		6 MFS Emerging Growth B	Large-cap Growth	87.62
		7 Oberweis Emerging Growth	Small-cap Growth	87.06
		8 American Century Ultra Inv	Large-cap Growth	86.45
		9 American Century Giftrust Inv	Mid-cap Growth	84.46
		10 Federated Kaufmann K	Mid-cap Growth	79.43
1992	**Value**			
		1 Oakmark I	Large-cap Value	48.90%
		2 Heartland Value	Small-cap Value	42.48
		3 Skyline Special Equities	Small-cap Value	42.41
		4 Fidelity Select Automotive	Mid-cap Value	41.62
		5 Oppenheimer Quest Cap Value A	Mid-cap Blend	40.99
		6 Parnassus	Mid-cap Blend	36.80
		7 Liberty Contrarian Sml Cap A	Small-cap Value	33.38
		8 UAM ICM Small Co	Small-cap Value	32.28
		9 Shelby	Mid-cap Growth	32.27
		10 AIM Mid Cap Equity A	Mid-cap Blend	31.74
1993	**Global**			
		1 GAM Global A	World Stock	74.73%
		2 Prudential Global Growth	World Stock	47.90
		3 PBHG Growth	Mid-cap Growth	46.71
		4 Morgan Stanley Inst Glb Value Eq A	World Stock	44.24
		5 Fidelity Select Industrial Equip	Large-cap Blend	43.33
		6 Oppenheimer Global A	World Stock	42.63
		7 American Heritage	World Stock	41.39
		8 Seligman Glb. Sml Co A	World Stock	40.09
		9 Excelsior Value & Restr	Large-cap Blend	39.95
		10 Fidelity Select Leisure	Large-cap Growth	39.55

Table 6.3   (Continued)

Year	Dominant Style	Fund Name	Category	Return
1994	**Growth**			
		1 PBHG Emerging Growth	Small-cap Growth	23.78%
		2 RS Value & Growth	Mid-cap Growth	23.11
		3 Montgomery Growth R	Large-cap Blend	20.91
		4 Deutsche Small Cap Invm	Small-cap Growth	19.31
		5 Strong Growth Inv	Large-cap Growth	17.27
		6 AIM Aggressive Growth A	Mid-cap Growth	17.19
		7 Franklin CA Growth A	Mid-cap Growth	16.53
		8 Janus Aspen Agg Growth Inst.	Mid-cap Growth	16.33
		9 Turner Mid-Cap Value	Mid-cap Value	16.03
		10 Janus Mercury	Large-cap Growth	15.86
1995	**Growth**			
		1 Alger Capital App B	Large-cap Growth	78.32%
		2 Perkins Opportunity	Small-cap Growth	70.29
		3 Turner Small-Cap Growth	Small-cap Growth	68.16
		4 Reserve Small-Cap Growth R	Small-cap Growth	67.46
		5 Shepherd Large Cap Growth	Mid-cap Growth	64.61
		6 TCW Galileo Small Cap Growth I	Mid-cap Growth	64.29
		7 Alger Small Cap Inst	Small-cap Growth	60.83
		8 Morgan Stanley Sp Growth B	Mid-cap Growth	60.21
		9 Fidelity Select Air Trans	Mid-cap Growth	59.54
		10 Wasatch Ultra Growth	Small-cap Growth	58.77
1996	**Growth**			
		1 Van Kampen Growth A	Mid-cap Growth	61.99%
		2 State Street Research Aurora A	Small-cap Value	56.57
		3 First American Micro Cap A	Small-cap Growth	55.84
		4 Phoenix-Engemann Sml & MidCap Gr A	Small-cap Growth	52.37
		5 Needham Growth	Mid-cap Growth	51.56
		6 Fremont U.S. Micro-Cap	Small-cap Growth	48.70
		7 Dreyfus Premier Growth & Income A	Large-cap Blend	48.63
		8 Wanger US Small Cap	Small-cap Growth	46.59
		9 MFS Core Growth A	Large-cap Growth	46.02
		10 Pacific Advisors Sml Cap A	Small-cap Blend	43.70

(Continued)

Table 6.3   (Continued)

Year	Dominant Style	Fund Name	Category	Return
1997	**Growth**			
		1 American Heritage	World Stock	75.00%
		2 Munder Micro-Cap Equity Y	Small-cap Growth	71.29
		3 FMI Focus	Small-cap Growth	69.75
		4 Hartford Capital Appreciation A	Mid-cap Growth	55.11
		5 Oakmark Select I	Mid-cap Value	55.02
		6 Brazos Small Cap Y	Mid-cap Growth	54.53
		7 MFS Strategic Growth A	Large-cap Growth	50.40
		8 SAFECO Growth Opp Inv	Small-cap Growth	49.97
		9 Gabelli Value A	Mid-cap Blend	48.23
		10 MFS Mass Inv Gr Stk A	Large-cap Growth	48.15
1998	**Growth**			
		1 ProFunds Ultra OTC Inv	Large-cap Growth	185.27%
		2 Grand Prix A	Mid-cap Growth	111.83
		3 Potomac OTC Plus Inv	Large-cap Growth	104.22
		4 Rydex OTC Inv	Large-cap Growth	86.61
		5 Transamerica Prem Aggr Growth Inv	Large-cap Growth	84.07
		6 Millennium Growth	Mid-cap Growth	84.06
		7 Transamerica Prem Growth Opp Inv	Mid-cap Growth	80.27
		8 Jundt Twenty-Five A	Large-cap Growth	74.89
		9 Janus Twenty	Large-cap Growth	73.39
		10 PBHG Large Cap 20 PBHG	Large-cap Growth	67.83
1999	**Growth**			
		1 Morgan Stanley Inst Sm Cap Growth	Small-cap Growth	313.91%
		2 Van Wagoner Emer Growth	Small-cap Growth	291.15
		3 Nevis Fund	Mid-cap Growth	286.53
		4 Van Wagoner Post-Venture	Small-cap Growth	237.22
		5 ProFunds Ultra OTC Inv	Large-cap Growth	232.01
		6 BlackRock Micro-Cap Equity Instl	Small-cap Growth	221.54
		7 Thurlow Growth	Mid-cap Growth	213.21
		8 Van Wagoner Small Cap Growth	Small-cap Growth	207.88
		9 Loomis Sayles Aggressive Growth Instl	Mid-cap Growth	198.75
		10 Strong Enterprise Inv	Mid-cap Growth	187.84

Table 6.3   (Continued)

Year	Dominant Style	Fund Name	Category	Return
2000	Blend			
		1 Schroder Ultra Inv	Small-cap Blend	147.70%
		2 American Eagle Capital Appre	Mid-cap Growth	84.67
		3 CRM Mid Cap Value Instl	Mid-cap Blend	55.55
		4 Century Small Cap Select Instl	Mid-cap Growth	54.95
		5 CGM Focus	Small-cap Blend	53.93
		6 Lord Abbett Mid-Cap Value A	Mid-cap Value	53.30
		7 New Alternatives	Small-cap Blend	51.76
		8 American Eagle Twenty	Large-cap Growth	49.66
		9 Fairholme Fund	Mid-cap Blend	46.54
		10 Bjurman Micro-Cap Growth	Small-cap Growth	45.57
2001	Value			
		1 Schroder Ultra Inv	Small-cap Blend	73.46%
		2 Ameristock Focused Value	Small-cap Value	60.42
		3 Corbin Small-Cap Value	Small-cap Value	53.66
		4 Wasatch Micro Cap	Small-cap Growth	49.99
		5 CGM Focus	Small-cap Blend	47.65
		6 Boston Partners Sm Cap Value II Inv	Small-cap Value	47.49
		7 Aegis Value	Small-cap Value	42.66
		8 Franklin MicroCap Value A	Small-cap Value	41.28
		9 Satuit Capital Micro Cap	Small-cap Blend	38.16
		10 FPA Capital (#1 over 11 years)	Small-cap Value	38.13

Source: Morningstar.

in the market, his performance will suffer. Put another way, when small-cap value stocks aren't doing so well, he won't look so hot. Ideally I prefer managers who do well whatever the market conditions. But some managers, like Bob, are so good at their discipline that I'll select them just for that. They're so good they know how to minimize loss in bad times.

Bob consistently invests in stocks that match his discipline, and he has done better than others over time. The market may fluctuate and go through cycles, but Bob stays with his discipline. He is a superior stock picker with staying power for over a decade. That is the kind of consistency I want and what I mean by picking the best player for every position. The overall allocation may be the most significant determinant of your game plan's performance, but, as I've said, you also need the best player possible in every allocated position in order to score.

Two other nuggets contained in the King of the World and King for a Year charts are:

1. *Consistent managers are crucial.* A long-term winner will almost always have a bad year or two. For instance, FPA Capital, the number one fund for the 11-year period, was down 0.42 percent in 1998 while several funds were up 20 percent or more. A careful analysis of that year would have told the investor that all small caps were getting hammered. A mutual fund manager who wanted to be in the top 10 list each year would have to radically shift style almost every year. That's a prescription for disaster.

2. *Diversification is key.* No single fund or style dominated the entire 11-year period (though various sized growth funds led in 7 out of 10 years, as the period was marked by up markets). But if you follow your diversified game plan and allocate to the best managers for each style, you will be more likely to achieve your goals.

Now that you've seen the rankings, try not to get hooked by the whole horse-racing aspect of fund performance. What do I mean by that? As you can see from these charts, in any given year there are many superior funds. In one year one is up, in another year it is down. Of course it's important that you find a top fund in the asset and style class you need. But if you have a diversified portfolio, you're like the owner of a great ball team. You've got excellent players who cover for one another when they have an off day or two. I would argue that it's a heck of a lot harder and more important to stick with a superior strategy than it is to find a superior fund. So don't let charts like these derail you from your game plan. Use them, but don't abuse them.

Deciding Which Funds to Buy and Hold

In order to know whether the fund you're considering measures up, you'll have to do some comparative analysis. This can be done easily on the Web with the help of Morningstar Quicktake® Reports at Morningstar. com.

The key data point you'll be looking for here is known as the total return, which reflects both growth in the share price of a fund and the value of any reinvested dividends or capital gains. This number reflects a fund's gains (or losses) over a given period of time. The one-, three-, five-, and ten-year returns are the terms that are typically compared.

Before I'll select a fund, the first thing I do is comparison shop its total returns against an appropriate benchmark index. I don't care how much buzz a manager generates, I don't even want to meet him or her until I make sure the fund's returns are up to snuff. Picking the right benchmark here is key; the choice depends on what you're measuring. For example, the Standard & Poor's 500 Index might be fine for a large-cap fund. But the Russell 2000 index, composed of smaller companies, would be a better choice to measure the performance of a small-cap fund.

In addition, you'll want to compare the fund's performance to those of its peers. You need to make sure you're comparing apples to apples—not tangerines. So if you're sizing up a mid-cap growth fund like Artisan MidCap you don't want to put it up against a large-cap value fund like Clipper. A better comparison would be Artisan MidCap to Calamos Growth, another mid-cap growth fund.

These comparisons can all be done relatively fast using the Fund Quickrank section on Morningstar.com. In addition, the Total Returns section of the Morningstar Quicktake® Report also provides a comparison of returns to average category performance as well as a comparison to an appropriate index.

If I'm going to invest with a fund, I like to see that the manager has beaten the fund's benchmark two out of three years and cumulatively over three years. He or she must also beat the benchmark three out of five years as well as cumulatively over five years. By doing these scans, I aim to compare not just overall performance, but how the fund managed in times of extremes, in both the up and down cycles. The funds I pick have to be in line with their benchmarks or outperform them in the market's good and bad years.

The down years are key. Protecting principal against loss is an extremely important part of any game plan. The key difficult years for stock funds of late have been 1987, 1990, 1994, 2000, 2001, and 2002. For bond funds the two years I check are 1994 and 1999. In 1994 bond funds were punished severely when the U.S. Federal Reserve raised its interest rates eight times. It was the worst year in bonds in my lifetime.

Don't ignore good years, though. They can be telling, too. For stock funds a prime year is 1999. For bond funds the rebound in 1995 was very impressive.

The best-case scenario would be to find a fund that doesn't go down as much as its benchmark in the bad years and outperforms in the good years. You won't find many funds that do this, but it's something to shoot for.

. . . And Knowing When to Fold

For years I was taught to avoid "timing." The ideal, I learned then, was to create an allocation strategy and portfolio in which you could buy and hold funds indefinitely. Early in my career I, too, spread what is often held to be the industry's gospel to my clients and anybody else who would listen. But real experience has taught me that investing—much like the rest of life—is not so simple.

I now believe that radical market fluctuations sometimes demand radical action. This means that there are not only times when you shouldn't buy and hold funds, but also times when you'll need to adjust your allocation. To hold on to an equity or bond fund in a prolonged down period (or up period without taking action to capture gains) is just not prudent. Such action isn't to be done on a whim. Most of the time it is a good idea to stay with an allocation that has been carefully constructed to meet your goals and take the appropriate amount of risk. But the markets won't always respect your carefully designed strategy.

So just when should you sell a fund or shift your allocation? To better understand this situation, let's consider how you might have handled two different funds in the very real volatility of 2000, the year the tech crash started. It was a year when the S&P 500 fell 10 percent, the Dow declined 6 percent and the tech-heavy Nasdaq dropped a painful 39 percent.

Let's assume you held both FPA Capital, a small-cap value fund, and Spectra, a large-cap growth fund. Both were among the top performers of the U.S. diversified group over an 11-year period shown in Table 6.2. In 2000, FPA reported a 3.1 percent loss while Spectra, ranked 16th out of 25 over 11 years, had a 32.5 percent loss.

In both cases I have great respect for the managers. Bob's consistent style we discussed earlier. The Spectra fund, on the other hand, had been managed by David Alger, an intelligent and highly respected growth investor whom I had the opportunity to meet in the green room at CNBC. After David tragically died in the World Trade Center attack of September 11, 2001, David's brother Fred came back from England to take over management of the fund. I have great respect for Fred but there are times when it doesn't matter who the manager is. During some volatile periods you just want to stop your losses.

Thus, in the case of FPA Capital and Spectra in 2000, you would have wanted to take two different approaches. You probably would have left your holding in FPA alone because it outperformed the market even though it was down. And you would probably have sold out of the Spectra fund, as its performance fell from the sizzling return of 72 percent in 1999 to a stunning loss of 32.5 percent the following year. Of the top 25 funds for 11 years it was down the most in 2000. Why? It was heavy in technology, so it really got clobbered.

Your Spectra holding in 2000 would have required you as the coach of your game plan to call two plays. The first would be a change in your overall allocation. (This is why it's called active allocation.) Let's assume you had put together the aggressive model portfolio in Chapter 5 and you picked the Spectra fund to fill the 10 percent large company growth slot. Once it became obvious that the growth style was no longer performing, you or your advisor would have needed to make a judgment call. In this case, I would have either reduced the growth allocation to 5 percent or eliminated growth altogether. The second play would be to take the physical action. That means selling Spectra (or trimming the holding) to meet your new allocation strategy.

If you had remained in Spectra, you would have been down 32 percent in 2000, 17 percent in 2001, and 31 percent through June 19, 2002.

This all may sound easy in hindsight, you say. But how do you know it's time for a change in allocation or fund holding? It is never clear-cut. But you might take heart in knowing that a well-diversified portfolio can cushion you against the need for an allocation shift except during extreme times. If you have enough allocated to safer asset categories such as bonds, small-cap value, or cash, you might have hedged your bets in 2000 or even scored without needing to make any changes.

In addition, if you keep informed, you may notice that some market shifts aren't always as sudden as they seem. In September 1999, six months before the tech crash, I thought technology funds were wildly overinflated. I said as much in a televised interview with Bill Griffeth on CNBC's "Power Lunch." I suggested that investors should think about getting out of tech for the first six months of the year 2000.

In the interest of full disclosure, I didn't go back to my office and pull everybody out of technology. What I did do was to review the 2000 allocation strategy for each client. Then I gradually adjusted allocation strategies where necessary and pulled back on aggressive growth funds.

Trying to tell you when to start selling is like a weather forecaster telling you what the weather will be three months in advance: nearly impossible. But I use both top-down and bottom-up barometers to judge the overall economy and specific funds.

The top-down assessment takes into account the general economic outlook and the status of business and laws that affect corporate spending and taxes. I also look at geopolitical events, listen to experts like

Warren Buffett and John Templeton, and consider consumer confidence indicators. Many of these factors are interrelated. For example, the steady drumbeat of corporate accounting scandals starting with Enron in 2001 had enormous implications for consumer confidence, which dropped like a rock.

The "bottom up" issue has to do with the mutual funds and managers themselves. A red flag goes up for me when I see the returns of a particular style of funds (e.g., small-cap growth or large-cap blend) eroding as a whole block or when a particular mutual fund's performance starts to deteriorate. If a style or manager is doing worse in comparison to like funds, I also take notice. When a fund drops 10 percent or 10 percentage points more than similar funds in any given year-to-date period, it is on my "concerned" list. When it drops between 15 and 20 percent, I generally sell it. The rest of a portfolio will generally make up for the loss to that point.

However, there are times when changes occur more rapidly, such as the "perfect storm" pattern of mid-2002. Here more drastic measures may be needed. During that period all equities were getting pounded and there was no place to go but bonds and cash. What I do with a portfolio during times like that also depends on clients' situations, their risk tolerances, their ages, how many other financial assets they have, and their goals. For clients who are suffering from too much risk we retreat to the bunker portfolio.

In mid-2002 some clients simply wanted out of the market until the crisis passed. Others were steadfast and eager to remain in funds that could grab stocks at what we hoped would turn out to be low prices. This optimistic group figured that if IBM was a good investment at $90 a share, it was a great one at $68. "Put some more money with the managers who are buying stuff so cheap!" they told me.

In each case, I always give clients my opinion and my recommendation based on their total situation and what I think will happen. I explain that there are two kinds of losses: loss of principal and loss of opportunity. The danger in lessening equity positions is that they won't have as many stock funds to benefit from when there is a rebound. That constitutes a loss of opportunity even though it protects principal. In bad times you want to minimize the other kind of loss—the loss of principal.

That is when you call a time-out in the game, and you get partially or totally out of the market.

Knowing when to buy and hold and when to fold is, as I've said before, more art than science. At the risk of sounding self-serving, I believe this is an area where the experience of a Certified Financial Planner can be of particular benefit. The best planners can offer you a more holistic and objective perspective on your financial situation and how it fits into the current investing climate. I'll discuss how to find a good advisor in more detail in Chapter 11.

How to Be a Star:
Using Morningstar's Rating System

You may be wondering whether you could just forget about those pesky benchmark and peer group comparisons we discussed earlier. Why not simply invest in funds that received the top four- or five-star billing from Morningstar? (To find a fund's Morningstar Rating™, go to its Quicktake® report on Morningstar.com and click on Ratings.)

You certainly can do that. A five-star top overall rating from Morningstar is nothing to sneeze at. For a fund to have a Morningstar Rating™ it must be in existence for over three years. Then Morningstar runs monthly analyses on all funds on a three-, five-, and ten-year trailing period and assigns a rating to each fund. The top 10 percent of a category get the enviable five stars, the next 22.5 percent get the four stars, the middle 35 percent get three stars, the next 22.5 percent get two stars, and the bottom 10 percent get one. Most of the funds I would use would have four or five stars.

But don't pick a fund solely on that basis. There could be some very good funds that are not rated at all because they lack the three-year track record required by Morningstar, even though the manager him- or herself is very experienced. Other funds may be flawed in some area that prevents them from garnering top billing but be worth your consideration anyway. What you want to do is build on the fund information you glean from the Morningstar Rating™ system.

Morningstar Rating™, which debuted in 1985, is best used as a screen that helps sift a confusing array of thousands of funds down to a more manageable pool from which you can choose. Morningstar used to assign stars in only four categories (domestic stock, international stock, taxable bond, and municipal bond). Now it rates funds in 48 Morningstar categories, enabling large-cap value funds to be compared to other large-cap value funds, for example. Comparisons are made to category-based peer groups.

This approach is helpful because it makes the rating system less sensitive to market movements. Prior to this system the four- and five-star ratings favored the categories of the market that were moving the most. This led to the "hot fund" syndrome and in some cases significantly distorted an otherwise effective allocation strategy.

Funds in all 48 categories now have an equal shot at top ratings. The rating system also identifies funds that are winners even though their style may be out of favor. That means a five-star fund may actually be showing losses but still have five stars because it is the best in its category.

The rating is all based on past history and it does not predict the future. Stars are only a starting point. Either you or your advisor needs to do more fundamental analysis of a fund's strategy and management to decide what the future prospects of a given fund might be. And of course you must consider how a fund fits into your portfolio and whether it matches your allocation needs.

Who Manages the Fund?

A manager is the decision maker of a fund. Managers make the final determination of when to invest in stocks or bonds and when it's time to bail out. Their actions ultimately determine whether you make or lose money. You want the cream of the crop. But how do you figure out who's on top?

For me, a manager's past performance is a critical element in determining whether you've found a winner. But the performance numbers of a fund don't tell the whole management story. Even if a manager has produced outstanding three- and five-year performance numbers, there's more I want to know.

Though there are always exceptions to the rules, I want someone with experience, someone who has been in the investment business for at least 15 years and who has been managing money for no less than 10 years. (Morningstar will give you a manager's tenure at a fund. You may need to call the fund company to find out more about the manager's background.) If this test means you rule out rookies with a "lucky hand," then so be it. You'll catch up with the rookie a few years down the line— if his or her "lucky hand" proves to be built on a solid foundation with staying power.

Not only do the years of experience give you a sense of a manager's consistency, but time also helps managers develop a disciplined approach to buying and selling stocks or bonds. A disciplined approach is another characteristic that I look for in managers. You want to choose managers who can clearly state what criteria they use to make their buy or sell decisions. For instance, you may want value managers who say that they buy a stock when they consider it to be at a 40 percent discount to its intrinsic value. You want them to be up-front about their approach and consistent in their actions. At the same time, you also want managers with an articulated exit strategy, or a way of handling the market when their style is out of favor. There is a fine line between commitment and blind allegiance to a losing proposition. Consistency is to be applauded, but purism at the investor's expense is to be avoided.

A good manager should take steps to save his or her other investors from getting skewered in a bad market. Is it always possible to do this? No. But an effort should be made. Bob Olstein, manager of the Olstein Financial Alert, managed to shift gears enough in his fund to provide investors with positive returns in up years like 1999 and down years like 2000 and 2001. While 2002 was a tougher year for him, he was still beating his peer group.

Information about a manager's discipline, while not as easily accessible as quantitative data, can be found in media interviews and often in fund reports as well. For some basic information on a manager's background, go to the Morningstar Quicktake® Report's "Fees & Management" section under the Portfolio toolbar.

When you're looking for managers who deliver consistency, you might wonder whether you can depend on a given fund family to deliver a predictable management strategy. Fund families offer a wide range of funds under one roof and name, such as Fidelity or Alliance. However, don't be lulled into thinking that the company's stability will deliver you returns through thick and thin. There are very few fund families with cultures strong enough to foster consistently good management. In fact, you need to guard against the opposite. That is, family funds can foster groupthink that is dangerous. Many Janus and Putnam funds have suffered in the post–bull market years in part because the families as a whole overemphasized technology.

For my taste, of the biggest families that have stood the test of time, the two I like the most are the American Funds and Vanguard. Both have proven to be ethical, competent, fair, and knowledgeable about running a solid and responsive organization of several funds. I've never had to apologize for anything they've done. Back in 1972 I put some of my clients into the venerable American Funds Investment Company of America and they're still in that investment. The fund posted 23 consecutive positive years until 2001, when it was down only 4.5 percent. Never having to say you're sorry is a big deal in this business!

Finally, two quick footnotes on the conflicts of interest that can dog the people and companies behind your funds. The first concerns fund managers who also manage private accounts, generally for high-net-worth individuals. These managers sometimes face potential problems

Demand Diversification

If the 401(k) plan of your employer permits you to invest in only one or two families of funds, consider taking some action to expand your options. Talk to your human resources administrator about getting a better 401(k) plan. A commitment to one way of investing is no way to achieve diversification. And in the end, diversification is the only way you can assure your financial future.

with conflicts of interest. For instance, when they find a good stock but can purchase only so many shares, do they put those shares into their private account or the mutual fund? And how do they handle stock sales? There has been at least one instance where a manager sold some losing stock from his private account to his mutual fund, for the benefit of the former and to the detriment of the latter.

It's hard to avoid all managers who handle private accounts. And some managers do take proactive steps to prevent jeopardizing the mutual fund's performance. It's a good idea to ask the customer service representative about the manager's policy about private accounts. If you're working with a good advisor, he or she should be aware of this issue.

My second point concerns the big brokerage houses that sell their own funds through their "captive" brokers. Many of the big brokerage firms have such funds. Just check out the mutual fund listings in any newspaper under such familiar names as American Express, Salomon Smith Barney, and Merrill Lynch. In many cases, though not all, you can buy these funds only from the companies themselves. I suggest you avoid this situation if you can. I don't like the idea that an investor is forced to go to a certain brokerage house to get a fund. The whole structure raises issues about incentives and potential conflicts of interest of the sales force. And big brokerage names don't always mean best funds. There are, of course, exceptions such as the Smith Barney Aggressive Growth Fund. This is the number-four fund on the list of top 25 U.S. diversified and world stock funds (see Table 6.2). Rich Freeman, its manager, held up very well in 2000 and 2001, even after an exceptional 1999. In 2002 the fund was down 32 percent through July 19.

What'll It Cost You? Risks and Fees

How Risky Is It?

We discussed personal risk tolerance in Chapter 2. Here we'll discuss the investment risk itself. The two are interrelated. As I've said before, just how much risk you'll want to take (or how risky a fund you should pick) depends on your overall financial situation and your personal risk tolerance. Both will help determine how you put together your investment game plan.

So part of picking the right funds is knowing how to size up the risk of the investment itself. If you're working with a Certified Financial Planner, he or she will spend significant time on this subject with you. If you're on your own, Morningstar's risk rating (accessible in a Morningstar Quicktake® Reports Ratings section) makes it a snap to quickly size up where a particular fund fits historically on the risk odometer. It's not easy to project that into the future, though.

As discussed in Chapter 5, your portfolio allocation should be your primary guide to choosing the proper risk level. If you're allocating to a conservative or moderate portfolio, avoid funds above the average risk range. If you're allocating to an aggressive portfolio, you might consider funds with above-average or high-risk ratings. But be careful. You should make sure aggressive funds account for no more than 20 percent of your aggressive portfolio—and less for moderate and conservative portfolios. Why? Because high-risk funds' gains may be good but they're typically temporary. To capture them, you'll need to monitor your funds so you'll know when to get out. As I've said with sectors, it's like playing with matches.

If you want to delve further into the quantitative numbers behind a particular fund's risk level, there's plenty of data to wade into. But the one yardstick I'd suggest you focus on is something called standard deviation. This number can give you a good feel for a given fund's potential for volatility.

The standard deviation of a fund addresses how much a fund's performance varies over time. The number comes from taking the degree of variance, the ups and downs, of a given fund and comparing that to its average returns over a given period (typically three and five years). You can find the trailing three-year standard deviation for any fund in its Morningstar Quicktake® Report in the Ratings section. (Remember that both the Morningstar Rating™ and standard deviation are based on past history. No one can predict the future.)

Generally speaking, higher-risk funds have higher standard deviation numbers. The benchmark standard deviation that is typically used for comparison purposes is that of the Vanguard 500 Index Fund, because the fund reflects the broader market. For the trailing three years through June 2002, the fund had a standard deviation of 15.57. By comparison, the number-one fund for 25 years, FPA Capital, has a standard deviation of 29.12 for the same three years.

But as with all the criteria that you can use to pick a fund, risk needs to be weighed against outcome. In the short run FPA may be more volatile than some funds, but it's been a consistent performer.

Once you figure out where a fund fits on the risk spectrum, you and/or your advisor need to decide whether it will help you meet your financial goals. For example, if you're using the aggressive portfolio model discussed in Chapter 5, a high-risk growth fund might be a solid component of the 32.5 percent growth allocation. But it would not belong in the conservative portfolio model, which has no place for high-risk funds.

In the end, you've got to consider the inherent risks of a given fund. But, most importantly, you've also got to be true to your portfolio allocation and your goals.

What Are the Fees?

While you pay more visible transaction fees for buying and selling stocks, the cost of owning a mutual fund is also real. Cost is always an important factor to consider, but it's especially so in difficult economic times when you don't have the padding of 10 or even 5 percent returns to cover your expenses. When returns are low or negative, expenses actually come out of the principal in your portfolio or funds. There are two main cost-related issues you need to reckon with, the expense ratio and the load. (For data go to the fund's Morningstar Quicktake® Report and click on the Fees and Expenses toolbar.)

Expense Ratio

The key element to measuring cost with any fund is its expense ratio. This number is a comparison of the expenses charged to a fund's assets. The base expense number in this equation includes everything from management fees to marketing to the postage needed to get prospectuses mailed out to fund holders like you.

The expense ratio is where the fund generates its profits. High expenses mean less money in the bank for you. If a fund's expenses are $1 million and it has assets valued at $100 million, it has an expense ratio of 1 percent. Expense ratios are not permanently fixed; they fluctuate depending on the amount of assets under management and expenses.

What are reasonable expenses? To give you an idea of what average fund expenses were in mid-2002, Morningstar indicated that U.S. diversified funds had an average expense ratio of 1.44 percent, foreign stock funds averaged 1.69 percent, and U.S. taxable bond funds averaged 1.02 percent. If you're unsure what the average is, look at a few other funds that share the same Morningstar category and see what their expense ratios are.

Ultimately you want a fund with an expense ratio at or below these averages. Even these average expenses are too high by my estimation, so it's important to keep your eyes on these numbers and review them just as you do your return rates. Try to pick funds with lower expenses, so long as you're not sacrificing superior returns.

In particular, bond fund expenses seem alarmingly high to me considering they generally offer lower returns than stock funds. Because of this, I recommend that you choose bond funds with expense ratios below the average. If you're particularly eager to crank down your funds' expenses, check out Vanguard and American Funds. They are focused on holding down costs.

Load versus No-Load

The load fund versus no-load fund debate is often painted in black and white, when there are shades of gray. A load is essentially a commission that is charged in exchange for financial advice. Many self-directed investors out and out object to paying a commission to invest in funds. They buy only no-load funds, and there are plenty of no-loads to choose from. For those willing to pay for advice, the load structure introduces another issue—conflict of interest. When the person advising you is required to sell the fund in order to be paid, then his or her incentive may not align with your interest as the investor.

So the problems with loads are twofold. Not only are they costly, sometimes 4, 5, 6 percent of your investment, but the very advice you are paying for can end up being useless because of the potential for conflict of interest or because the representative you're dealing with is incompetent.

So where's the gray? There are some excellent funds that carry loads and there are still some excellent advisors who work on a commission. Many of my favorite funds are loads, such as Pimco Total Return and Thornburg Value.

In fact, load funds accounted for 16 out of the top 25 funds in the ranking of returns from 1991 through 2001 (see Table 6.2). FPA Capital and Calamos Growth, both load funds, took the top two spots. (These returns are based on pure performance and are not load-adjusted.)

Why would a company structure its funds to carry a load? Regardless of how good a fund is, it still needs to be sold. A load motivates a sales force to pay attention to a fund and promote it to investors. In a marketplace of thousands of funds, that's a huge benefit.

Before you rule out a load fund, consider a few things. If it's being recommended by an advisor who would be paid a load (and if you're not sure, ask), scrutinize the advice you're receiving. Ask for an ample range of fund choices to be sure the advisor is not simply favoring the fund that will pay him or her the biggest commission. Insist on seeing the track record of the fund to ensure that it stands on its own merits.

Also, don't forget to look at the big picture. If you have an advisor, ask him or her to explain how it fits into your overall game plan. If you're on your own, make sure it fits into your allocation strategy.

Finally, focus in on the expense ratio. A load fund with low annual expenses can actually be a good deal. For example, if you decide to invest $20,000 in a load fund with an up-front load of 5 percent, you'll pay $1,000 just to get your money invested. But if you remain in that fund for eight years, assuming no growth and with an annual expense ratio of 0.75 percent, you'd have $17,889 left. If instead you put that $20,000 in a no-load fund for eight years, again assuming no growth, but with an annual expense ratio of 1.44 percent, you'd have $17,808 left after eight years. Even if the performance is the same in the load and no-load funds over eight years, you're ahead of the game if the expenses in the load fund are low enough. In this example, eight years is the crossover point where the load fund is ahead because of lower expenses.

When deciding on a load fund, you'll also want to consider how long you expect to be invested. I know it isn't possible to accurately predict the future, but you need to take your expectations into account. That's because there are different types of shares that affect how and when you pay the loads and the expenses. Class A shares generally charge something called a front-end load of between 3 and 6 percent. This is an up-front charge that is lopped off your initial investment *before* it goes into the fund.

By contrast, Class B shares carry something called back-end loads, also known as contingent deferred sales charges. Here you're essentially encouraged to stay in the fund longer because the load charge that you would pay when selling declines each year you are in the fund. So you'll pay a high price (up to 6 percent of your investment value) if you pull your money out in the first year but that load generally drops to zero if you're willing to stick with the fund for between four and eight years.

What I don't like about Class B shares is that they distort your incentives: If you're disappointed in a manager and are inclined to sell, you may find yourself reluctant because you don't want to face the higher load for early exit—when in fact even with what is, in essence, a penalty you'd be better off out of there.

Class C shares generally charge what's known as a level load—an extra annual fee for the life of the investment. Generally the extra fee amounts to 1 percent that is paid to an advisor. This is another way of paying a fee to an advisor so be sure you're getting your money's worth for continued good advice. Otherwise, the fees are just eating up your returns without giving you any value added.

Finally, all of this load mumbo jumbo may not concern you at all if you are working with an advisor who charges an annual fee based on a percentage of your assets—an advisor like myself.

I have the luxury of getting load funds for my clients with no loads because many of these funds waive their commissions for professional advisors. In fact, about half of my favorite fund managers manage load funds. As an investor, you should take this into account when considering whether to hire an independent advisor on a fee basis. It's much better that a fee come from you than a mutual fund company in the form of a load, because your advisor will feel more accountable to you—it puts you both on the same side of the table.

Which Stocks Is My Manager Buying?

The mutual fund press pushes investors to focus in on which stocks their manager is buying as a way of assessing the value of a fund. I think it's important but overdone. What good would it do to look at stocks in a portfolio if you don't know much about stocks? As far as I'm concerned, one of the main benefits of mutual funds is that you don't have to get involved with stock picking. That's what you hire a manager for. And even if you were interested in getting involved in the micro-details of the fund's stock picks, it would not be an easy thing to do.

It's very difficult for the average investor to get enough information to know whether the manager is on target about any single stock pick. If Cisco is tanking you may be horrified to learn that your fund owns it. However, if the fund manager bought in at or near the low, he or she might be approaching it as a value play. Or your manager might have sold right before it tanked, even though the most recent (and often outdated) fund holding reports show Cisco still in the fund's portfolio. In either of these scenarios, you've given yourself heartburn for nothing. Unfortunately, this is an area that gets heavy coverage from the press—too heavy, in my opinion.

Don't waste your time second-guessing your fund manager on a stock-by-stock basis. It is better to look at the bigger picture that the stock holdings represent—the sector or industry weightings. (Look in the Portfolio section of the fund's Morningstar Quicktake® Report.) If you're choosing a fund for your offense or defense (rather than a special team), choose a fund that invests in four or more sectors. In addition, you'll generally want to select funds with at least 40 stocks for diversification purposes but less than 200. Any more than 200 stocks and you may find yourself paying the higher expenses of an actively managed fund in return for what amounts to an index fund. If you really want to purchase a fund with fewer than 40 stocks, you should exercise caution and invest a limited amount of assets into what is most likely a concentrated and high-risk fund.

A final consideration for stock picks is the turnover rate. This measurement is expressed as the percentage of stocks that are sold in a year's time. That means a fund with a 100 percent turnover ratio sells all its stocks in the given year while one with a 40 percent turnover ratio would sell all its stocks in about two and a half years.

The conventional wisdom holds that high turnover rates are no-nos because they lead to higher expenses in the form of trading costs and taxes. I agree that turnover can be a concern and typically prefer to see turnover rates around 40 percent or less. But for the most part turnover rates are like stock selection—I prefer to focus on results more than process.

Some of the best managers have very high turnover rates. A good manager can use buys and sells to offset tax implications, and in volatile markets can move fast to lock in gains or avoid further losses. For instance, Olstein Financial Alert has a turnover of 107 percent as of mid-year 2002 but taxes and expenses didn't hold back the stellar performance.

Getting the Facts . . . and More

Now that I've discussed the criteria I use for selecting the funds for my clients, let's consider how you can get this information yourself if you're not working with an advisor. (Your advisor should have access to significant data and resources. The information created specifically for professionals is often more in-depth than that which is available to individuals.) Much of the raw data is easily available on various excellent web sites such as Morningstar.com and Kiplinger.com. (Alternately, you can access Morningstar reports in the newsletter *Morningstar Mutual Funds*, which can be found in your local library.)

> ### *Hayden Play:*
> ### Hit the books (or the Internet).
>
> If you're a new investor, learn the difference between a stock, a bond, and a commodity. Once you have the basics down, there's always more to learn. Read good investment books, learn to distinguish between a sales pitch and sound advice, and then invest in what you know and whom you know. Whether you're a do-it-yourselfer or a client, homework pays off.

Questions related to qualitative matters such as a manager's philosophy may require a little more legwork. It starts with a call to the fund company. Most funds have an 800 telephone number (you can find this on the fund's Morningstar Quicktake® Report). When you call, identify yourself as a potential investor with some questions about how the fund works. Beyond the specific issues in question, you'll receive the added bonus of getting a feel for the responsiveness of the company that is handling your investment.

Additionally, the press can be helpful. From Internet analysts to mainstream media, thousands of mutual fund stories are published each year. Morningstar, TheStreet.com, and the *Wall Street Journal* are some of the top sources, but a Google search of the Internet can turn up many others. Just be cautious, because the majority of people who do the writing have never managed money or worked with clients. The quantitative information can be helpful, but without the insights of experience that added wisdom just isn't there.

Step 6, Pick the Players: Summing Up

Step 6 is about picking the right fund for your allocation needs and your financial goals. As you do your research, keep grounded and don't be swayed by the latest and greatest. You can use the questions in the following box to help you get started.

Top 10 Questions to Ask When Selecting Your Funds
(and Where to Find Answers)

1. Does the fund match a specific style within your overall allocation strategy? (Check your overall game plan as developed in Chapter 5.)

2. How has the fund performed over one, three, and five years in comparison to its peers? (Go to www.Morningstar.com for the fund's Quicktake® Report and click on Returns.)

3. How did the fund's performance compare to the appropriate benchmarks in 1999, 2000, 2001, and 2002? (Go to the fund's Quicktake® Report and click on Returns.)

4. Who is the manager and how long has he or she managed the fund? (Go to the fund's Quicktake® Report and click on Portfolio and then Management toolbars.)

5. Does the manager have at least 15 years of experience in the business and at least 10 years of experience actually managing money? (Call the mutual fund sales representative, and research past articles in the press.)

6. Does the manager agree with Morningstar's fund style category? If not, why? (Call the mutual fund sales representative, and read the press.)

7. What is the fund's annual expense ratio and/or load (if there is one)? (Go to the fund's Quicktake® Report and click on Portfolio and then Fees and Expenses toolbars.)

8. Is the fund's annual expense ratio lower than the average for its fund category? (Go to the fund's Quicktake® Report and click on Portfolio and then Fees and Expenses toolbars.)

9. How risky is the fund? See standard deviation and Morningstar risk rating. (Go to the fund's Quicktake® Report and click on Ratings.)

10. How many sectors does it hold? How many stocks does it hold? (Go to fund's the Quicktake® Report and click on Portfolio, or for updated information call the mutual fund sales representative.)

Chapter 7

Step 7: Know Your Team

In the preceding two chapters, you learned about the three levels of allocation—asset classes, fund styles, and specific funds. In this chapter I choose specific mutual funds to fill out the allocations. I've selected some of the funds I like and allocated them according to the four model portfolios to match the capitalization levels and styles we've already discussed. You'll recall that the models are the conservative, the moderate, the aggressive, and the bunker that were discussed in Chapter 5.

As of this writing, I believe the mutual funds I chose for the sample portfolios and their mutual fund managers are some of the best in the business. But this book is not about recommending the so-called "best" mutual funds or managers. I can't emphasize enough that you shouldn't conclude that these exact portfolios or mutual funds are ones that can fit everyone's needs. I am only using them to illustrate the process you should use with an advisor to get to know your team.

Why can't I prescribe the perfect fund to fit your needs for the long haul? Because there are too many variables that change all too fast. At any time a manager could leave or burn out. Or a fund could close. For example, years ago FPA Paramount, managed by Bill Sams, and Fidelity's Advisor Growth Opportunities fund, managed by George Vanderheiden, were two of my favorite funds. But over the years the funds' performances slipped, and both managers eventually retired from their posts. I no longer use these funds.

So instead of giving you reams of names and numbers that will soon be past their freshness date, I've given you guidelines about how to pick a good fund. Now I'll show you how to check whether you've assembled these funds into a team that will work together to meet your goals and address your risk tolerance.

By doing this before you invest your money, you'll be able to gauge whether the portfolio you've chosen will work for you. My point here is to give you an idea of how your specific fund choices and allocations will affect the risk you're taking on and the return you hope to get.

Think back to the idea of getting a suit fitted. Step 7 would be that second trip back to the tailor. You've already ordered the alterations to make the suit or dress is the perfect fit. Now it's time to try it on and make sure the measurements were correct.

Running the Data

Just how do you assess the strength of a total portfolio? This is an area that involves some number crunching, so it can be easier if you have an advisor. Not only do they have experience, but advisors also have easy access to software that will enable you to get a sense for how a particular group of funds would have worked together in the past.

For example, I use Morningstar® Principia® software. What I do is plug in the fund symbols and allocation levels—the percentage any fund contributes to the total portfolio. The software then synthesizes all the funds' past performances and develops a wide range of data ranging from the overall portfolio's risk level to its best and worst one-year period.

This data helps me and my clients understand the level of risk and reward that comes with their choices. It's important to remember this is a snapshot of how the portfolio operated in the past. Unfortunately, they still haven't developed any software to enable investors to predict the future. But looking at how a portfolio performs historically is a good way to get your bearings.

With today's computers, there's almost no limit to the information you can get about your portfolios. But unless you're one of those rare

> ### Crunching the Numbers on Your Own
>
> If you're a do-it-yourselfer dedicated to having command over the full complement of data tools, check with your local library to see if it has Morningstar® Principia® software. Alternately, you can purchase Principia directly from Morningstar. The price is steep but the information provided can be very useful. Still, much of the data you need to do a good analysis can be picked up from other less expensive sources online.

investors who has figured out how to get by with barely any sleep, you'll need to focus on a selection of important data. In Table 7.1 (Ghost of your Portfolio's Past) I've chosen some of the most important information I like to pull from the computer on a portfolio before I make a final decision.

This is information includes:

- *Basic Returns*. No surprise here. As you may have already noticed, the three most important criteria are performance, performance, and performance. So I run a comparison of the total returns for the portfolio as a whole for three months, one year, three years, five years, and ten years. In this chapter, all returns for multiple years are average annual returns. This is very important because the composite return gives you a feel for how effective the portfolio's diversification will be in changing markets. The returns shown in this chapter are historical through June 30, 2002.
- *Highs and Lows*. This section analyzes a portfolio's best and worst performances over various time periods. It gives you a feel for how volatile the portfolio is and also what type of markets (bull or bear) it favors. It's important to be aware that these periods are determined on what is called a rolling basis. That means it compares many more 12-month periods than it would if it were simply comparing calendar years. That's because it checks not only January through December but also February through January,

Table 7.1 Ghost of Your Portfolio's Past

	Bunker	Conservative*	Moderate	Growth	S&P 500	Nasdaq
3-Month return	-1.16%	-1.90%	-4.70%	-6.70%	-13.39%	-20.71%
1-Year return	7.81	4.67	0.47	-3.87	-17.98	-32.28
3-Year return	9.12	10.17	10.03	9.72	-9.17	-18.33
5-Year return	8.81	11.26	13.26	14.59	3.66	0.29
10-Year return	9.27	11.41	13.27	15.53	11.42	10.01
1-Year best return	17.40%	23.35%	31.16%	39.57%		
1-Year worst return	-2.43	0.25	-2.21	-8.80		
3-Year best return	12.74	17.22	20.54	27.20		
3-Year worst return	6.45	9.28	10.03	9.72		
3-Year standard deviation	3.22%	6.84%	11.32%	15.37%		
5-Year standard deviation	3.73	7.78	12.33	16.68		

Bull market: January 1991 to March 2000
Bear market: March 2000 to June 2002

Note: This table shows the historical performance of model portfolios as compared to market benchmarks. All multiyear data are average annual performances. Data is as of January 1 through June 30, 2002.
Source: Morningstar.

March through February, and so forth. It is a much more thorough way to measure performance than just using calendar years.

- *Standard Deviation.* As I discussed earlier, this is one of the best ways to judge a fund's risk. It gives an idea of how far up or down a fund's return moves from its normal historical range. The standard deviation works similarly for portfolios as a whole. Remember, the lower the number, the less volatile the portfolio. This information may be easier to digest if you look at the scatter plot included in the subsections on each portfolio.

Now we'll take a look at the third level of allocation for each of the model portfolios.

Conservative Portfolio

Earlier we discussed how this conservative game plan uses the offense and defense roughly equally with 50 percent allocated to stocks (see Table 7.2) and 40 percent allocated to high-quality bonds (see Table 7.3). The remaining 10 percent of the portfolio is allocated to what I call opportunistic cash. The portfolio is designed to be well balanced and to help control risk. Now let's consider how the portfolio fared using actual funds.

As you can see in Table 7.4, the conservative portfolio outperformed the benchmark index (here I'm using the S&P 500) except over the 10-year period. (The percentage point difference on the benchmark return line reflects the degree to which the fund either outperformed or underperformed its benchmark. For example, on a three-month basis it outperformed the S&P by 11.49 percent, whereas it underperformed by –0.01 percent on a 10-year basis.) That's because most of the past 10 years have been bull markets, a veritable heyday for more aggressive portfolios. Still, even then the portfolio would have made you money, just not as much as you might have made with a more aggressive portfolio.

Let's put that return in the context of how much risk you would have had to take. As you can see in Table 7.5, the conservative portfolio's standard deviation rate was less than half that of the S&P. So by choosing this conservative portfolio rather than parking your money in a

Table 7.2 Conservative Model/Stock Funds 50 Percent

	Value	*Blend*	*Growth*	*Total*
Large-cap	Clipper 10%	Thornburg Value 5%	0%	**15%**
Medium-cap	Olstein Financial Alert 10% First Eagle SoGen Global 10%	Oakmark Equity & Income 7.5%	0%	**27.5%**
Small-cap	Royce Low Price Stock 7.5%	0%	0%	**7.5%**
Total	**37.5%**	**12.5%**	**0%**	**50%**

benchmark index fund, you'd be getting better or similar returns than the benchmark with 50 percent less risk. Not a shabby deal, so long as you aren't banking on outsized returns to meet your goals.

A comparison of the risk/reward characteristics of any portfolio is made easier by the graph in Figure 7.1 (page 158). Morningstar calls this a scatter plot. The horizontal axis represents the three-year standard deviation while the vertical axis shows the three-year mean return. The scatter plots are divided into four quadrants. Funds or portfolios plotted

Table 7.3 Conservative Model/Fixed Income 40 Percent

	Short-Term	Intermediate-Term	Long-Term	Total
High-quality	SIT U.S. Gov. Secs. 10% Vanguard Infl. Prot. Secs. 10%	FPA New Income 10% Harbor Bond 10%	0%	40%
Medium-quality	0%	0%	0%	0%
Low-quality	0%	0%	0%	0%
Total	20%	20%	0%	40%

Table 7.4 Conservative Portfolio Historical Returns through June 30, 2002

	3-Month	1-Year	3-Year	5-Year	10-Year
Portfolio return	−1.90%	4.67%	10.17%	11.26%	11.41%
+/− Benchmark return	11.49	22.65	19.35	7.59	−0.01

Source: Morningstar. All multiyear data are average annual returns.

Table 7.5 **Conservative Portfolio Standard Deviation versus S&P 500 through June 30, 2002**

	3 Years		5 Years	
	Portfolio	*S&P 500*	*Portfolio*	*S&P 500*
Standard deviation	6.84	15.56	7.78	18.78

Source: Morningstar.

within the various quadrants can be characterized depending on where they end up on the graph:

Lower left: lower risk, lower return.
Lower right: higher risk, lower return.
Upper right: higher risk, higher return.
Upper left: lower risk, higher return.

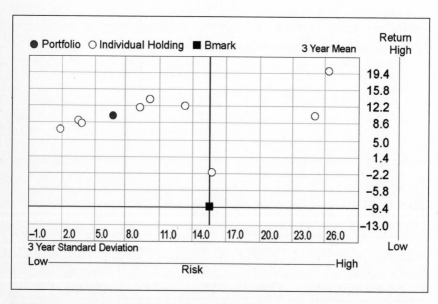

Figure 7.1 **Conservative Portfolio Scatter Plot**
Source: Morningstar.

Whenever I choose funds to fit a particular allocation, I check the results against such a scatter plot until the appropriate synergy for my client is reflected. It is not a foolproof way of creating a portfolio, but it is another tool that definitely helps.

In the conservative scatter plot you can see that the individual mutual fund holdings are mostly located in the upper-left quadrant of the graph, as is the gray circle that represents the portfolio as a whole. Not the highest return possible but lower risk—a good place for a conservative investor.

Finally I analyze the best and worst time periods for performance (see Table 7.6). This is important because it gives you a good feel for how volatile the portfolio is. All numbers for three years are compounded annually.

How do you put this information to use? Consider the worst performance as an acid test of your risk tolerance. In the case of any portfolio, ask yourself if you could sleep at night during the worst period for the returns. In the case of the conservative portfolio, that would have been a quarter where the portfolio was down 7.78 percent. If you feel you can (and you may be reassured to know that the S&P 500 was down substantially more than this), then this portfolio may be for you.

If you still are not sure about the degree of risk you can tolerate, I

Table 7.6 It Was the Best of Times, It Was the Worst of Times—Conservative Portfolio

	3 Months	
Best	May 1997 through July 1997	9.75%
Worst	June 1998 through August 1998	−7.78
	1 Year	
Best	April 1997 through March 1998	23.35
Worst	February 1994 through January 1995	0.25
	3 Years	
Best	April 1995 through March 1998	17.22
Worst	September 1993 through August 1996	9.28

Source: Morningstar. Multiyear data are average annual performances.

Hayden Play:
Protect the principal.

Hang on to the money you already have. That's the first rule of investing. Some loss some of the time is pretty inevitable in the stock market. But the best money managers limit injury to your portfolio and prevent unnecessary losses. In evaluating a mutual fund or even the performance of your overall portfolio, pay close attention to how the fund or portfolio fared in down years relative to its benchmark. It's more important that managers do better than the market on the downside than whether they outperform on the upside.

suggest you start with a conservative portfolio. Remember, the number-one rule of investing is to not lose principal. The number-two rule is to remember number one. Starting at a lower risk level will help you follow the rules.

Moderate Portfolio

The moderate game plan offers the investor some middle ground. You'll have a much stronger offense with 65 percent in equities, an increase of 15 percent over the more conservative. That leaves 35 percent on the defensive side, which is still a good cushion in a down market. (See Tables 7.7 and 7.8.)

Notice anything similar about the fund names? In fact, many are the same ones that I used in the conservative portfolio. Once I find a good fund I'm not shy about suggesting that all my clients use it. The difference for each portfolio comes in how much is allocated to it.

So as I shift gears from the conservative to the moderate portfolio, I trimmed the amount in bonds (from 10 percent down to 5 percent for the SIT U.S. Government Securities and Vanguard Inflation Protected Securities). I used that money to make a 17.5 percent investment in two growth funds. Growth funds were not a component of the conservative

Table 7.7   Moderate Model/Stock Funds 65 Percent

	Value	Blend	Growth	Total
Large-cap	Clipper 5% Oakmark 5%	Thornburg Value 10%	0%	20%
Medium-cap	Olstein Financial Alert 10% First Eagle SoGen Global 10%	0%	Hartford Midcap 10%	30%
Small-cap	Royce Low Price Stock 7.5%	0%	FMI Focus 7.5%	15%
Total	37.5%	10%	17.5%	65%

portfolio. If I had used this portfolio over the past 10 years I would have done well over the long term, as evidenced in Table 7.9.

Let's put those returns in context by comparing the moderate portfolio's historical returns to those of the conservative portfolio (see Table 7.10). In doing so, it becomes clear that their performances over the short and long term were largely dictated by overall market conditions. From March 2000 until July 2002, the bears triumphed. For 10 straight years prior to that time, the bulls were in charge.

Table 7.8 **Moderate Model/Fixed Income 25 Percent**

	Short-Term	*Intermediate-Term*	*Long-Term*	*Total*
High-quality	SIT U.S. Gov. Secs. 5% Vanguard Infl. Prot. Secs. 5%	FPA New Income 7.5% Harbor Bond 7.5%	0%	**25%**
Medium-quality	0%	0%	0%	**0%**
Low-quality	0%	0%	0%	**0%**
Total	**10%**	**15%**	**0%**	**25%**

Table 7.9 **Moderate Portfolio Historical Returns through June 30, 2002**

	3-Month	*1-Year*	*3-Year*	*5-Year*	*10-Year*
Portfolio return	−4.70%	0.47%	10.03%	13.26%	13.27%
+/− S&P 500	8.68	18.45	19.20	9.59	1.85

Source: Morningstar. Multiyear data provided are average annual performances.

Table 7.10   It Was the Best of Times, It Was the Worst of Times—Moderate Portfolio

	3 Months	
Best	September 1998 through November 1998	13.44%
Worst	June 1998 through August 1998	−11.00
	1 Year	
Best	April 1997 through March 1998	31.16
Worst	October 2000 through September 2001	−2.21
	3 Years	
Best	April 1997 through March 2000	20.54
Worst	July 1999 through June 2002	10.03

Source: Morningstar. Multiyear returns provided are average annual performances.

Because fixed income performs better than equities in a bear market, the conservative portfolio bested the moderate portfolio over the one- and three-year terms because its bond holdings acted almost as an offense (see Table 7.10). But over the five- and ten-year periods that were bullish, the moderate portfolio triumphed by about two percentage points. The moderate did better in a bull market.

In every up period, the moderate portfolio's best times outperform the conservative's best. For example, its one-year best was 31.2 percent compared with the conservative's one-year best of 23.4 percent. It should be this way, because the moderate has more offense. However, in difficult times the moderate portfolio, as you remember, has fewer defenses to cushion blows. So the lows are lower. The moderate's worst one-year return was a loss of 2.2 percent compared with the conservative's 0.25 percent gain.

The standard deviation for this portfolio is substantially higher than that of the conservative one or nearly double on both a three-year and five-year basis (see Table 7.11). That means that the moderate portfolio is riskier and more volatile to buy than the conservative one, but still not more so than the S&P 500 Index.

As you can see in the scatter plot (Figure 7.2), all of this portfolio's funds are in the northernmost quadrants—though they are almost evenly divided on the left and the right side (higher risk on the right

Table 7.11 Moderate Portfolio Standard Deviation versus S&P 500 through June 30, 2002

	3 Years		5 Years	
	Portfolio	*S&P 500*	*Portfolio*	*S&P 500*
Standard deviation	11.32	15.56	12.33	18.78

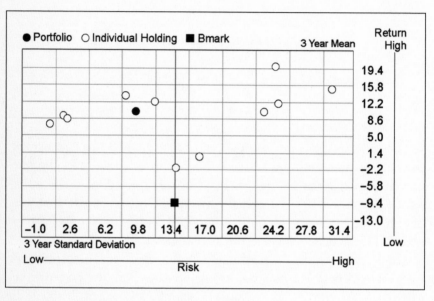

Figure 7.2 Moderate Portfolio Scatter Plot
Source: Morningstar.

side). But the composite total of the portfolio is in the top left quadrant—lower risk, higher return. As I've said before, these are conditions that suit the majority of investors.

Aggressive Portfolio

Now, the aggressive portfolio presents a game plan that gets a little more dramatic than many people may want (see Tables 7.12 and 7.13). We are increasing the power of the offense to a full 80 percent and scal-

Table 7.12   Aggressive Model/Stock Funds 80 Percent

	Value	Blend	Growth	Total
Large-cap	Oakmark 10%	Thornburg Value 10%	Growth Fund of America 10%	**30%**
Medium-cap	Olstein Financial Alert 10% First Eagle SoGen Global 10%	0%	Hartford Midcap 7.5% Calamos Growth 7.5%	**35%**
Small-cap	Royce Low Price Stock 7.5%	0%	FMI Focus 7.5%	**15%**
Total	**37.5%**	**10%**	**32.5%**	**80%**

ing defense back to only 20 percent. Investors in this portfolio are hoping for higher highs.

During down markets, growth investors feel the pain of their risk taking. This is evidenced by the three-month and one-year returns (actually losses) on this portfolio shown in Table 7.14. You need to be prepared to handle this if you're going to pick an aggressive portfolio.

The aggressive portfolio is still beating the S&P 500 Index by a significant margin in all the historical returns. This is as it should be. I don't prescribe ultra-aggressive portfolios—all stocks—because I am always

Table 7.13 Aggressive Model/Fixed Income 15 Percent

	Short-Term	Intermediate-Term	Long-Term	Total
High-quality	Vanguard Infl. Prot. Secs. 5%	FPA New Income 5% Harbor Bond 5%	0%	15%
Medium-quality	0%	0%	0%	0%
Low-quality	0%	0%	0%	0%
Total	5%	10%	0%	15%

Table 7.14 Aggressive Portfolio Historical Returns through June 30, 2002

	3-Month	1-Year	3-Year	5-Year	10-Year
Portfolio return	−6.70%	−3.87%	9.72%	14.59%	15.53%
+/− S&P 500	6.69	14.11	18.90	10.93	4.11

Source: Morningstar. Multiyear data provided are average annual performances.

careful to do my best to make sure that the risks I take don't put my principal at risk. My aggressive portfolio has bonds, and most of the stock funds are fairly conservative as well. As I see it, nearly all well-diversified portfolios should beat the S&P 500 because that index has no fixed-income component to cushion down markets. It is essentially a pure growth index. (However, as a bull market favoring growth roared throughout much of the past 10 years, the conservative and bunker portfolios underperformed the S&P 500 Index over that period.)

The best and worst time periods for the aggressive portfolio (see Table 7.15) reflect the wider ranges of returns that an aggressive investor needs to be able to handle. This charged portfolio far outperformed the others in up periods but significantly underperformed them in down periods. Sure, that 39.6 percent 12-month return from the bull market's hey day looks great. But can you stomach a 14.2 percent loss that you would have had in the summer of 1998? If not, take a pass on this model.

The volatility of the aggressive portfolio approaches that of the S&P 500 Index on both a three- and five-year basis (see Table 7.16). The scatter plot in Figure 7.3 brings that higher volatility into focus.

The majority of the funds are located in the upper-right quadrant, signifying a higher-risk, higher-return group of funds. Even the portfolio as a whole sits on the dividing line between lower risk and higher risk. That's about as far to the right as I ever suggest a portfolio should go.

Table 7.15   **The Best and Worst of the Aggressive Portfolio's Times**

	3 Months	
Best	October 1998 through December 1998	17.85%
Worst	June 1998 through August 1998	−14.16
	1 Year	
Best	April 1999 through March 2000	39.57
Worst	October 2000 through September 2001	−8.80
	3 Years	
Best	April 1997 through March 2000	27.20
Worst	July 1999 through June 2002	9.72

Source: Morningstar. Multiyear data provided are average annual performances.

Table 7.16   Aggressive Portfolio Standard Deviation versus S&P 500 through June 30, 2002

	3 Years		5 Years	
	Portfolio	*S&P 500*	*Portfolio*	*S&P 500*
Standard deviation	15.37	15.56	16.68	18.78

Source: Morningstar.

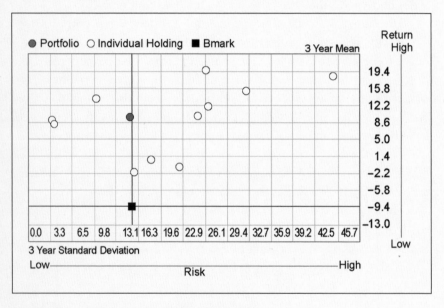

Figure 7.3   Aggressive Portfolio Scatter Plot
Source: Morningstar.

Bunker Portfolio

The idea for the bunker portfolio came at the height of the bear market in 2002. Some people were really scared, especially in July when the market dropped about 8 percent in a single month. The bottom was falling out from under a number of individual stocks. New clients were asking what I would do with new money. Even a conservative portfolio didn't offer enough security for some people.

Table 7.17 **Bunker Model/Stock Funds 30 Percent**

	Value	*Blend*	*Growth*	*Total*
Large-cap	Clipper 10%	0%	0%	10%
Medium-cap	First Eagle SoGen Global 10%	Oakmark Equity & Income 10%	0%	20%
Small-cap	0%	0%	0%	0%
Total	20%	10%	0%	30%

So I created a safer portfolio. (See Tables 7.17 and 7.18.) What did it entail? It ratcheted up the fixed-income component (defense) to 55 percent from the conservative portfolio's 40 percent. But even the stock funds were chosen to provide defense. How? All three of the funds used for this example are so-called hybrid funds.

Hybrids are one of a bear market investor's best friends. They are comprised of a mix of bonds, stocks and cash. Essentially, we leave it up to these managers to make the allocation call. During down markets these funds tend to be heaviest in bonds and cash. To the extent they

Table 7.18   Bunker Model/Fixed Income 55 Percent

	Short-Term	*Intermediate-Term*	*Long-Term*	*Total*
High-quality	SIT U.S. Gov. Secs. 15% Vanguard Infl. Prot. Secs. 15%	FPA New Income 12.5% Harbor Bond 12.5%	0%	**55%**
Medium-quality	0%	0%	0%	0%
Low-quality	0%	0%	0%	0%
Total	30%	25%	0%	55%

own stocks, these funds buy shares on a value basis at a very big discount. The historical returns in Table 7.19 give you a feel for the steady returns the portfolio has had.

The best and worst time periods in Table 7.20 underscore the fact that the real benefits of a bunker approach come in the tough years. No double-digit losses here. But the double-digit gains never exceed 20 percent. The bunker essentially holds down your investment fort.

Table 7.19   Bunker Portfolio Historical Returns through June 30, 2002

	3-Month	1-Year	3-Year	5-Year	10-Year
Portfolio return	−1.16%	7.81%	9.12%	8.81%	9.27%
+/− S&P 500	13.79	29.79	19.97	7.93	−0.50

Source: Morningstar. Multiyear data provided are average annual performances.

Table 7.20   The Bunker Best and Worst of Times

	3 Months	
Best	May 1997 through July 1997	6.49%
Worst	June 1998 through August 1998	−2.43
	1 Year	
Best	March 2000 through February 2001	17.40
Worst	February 1994 through January 1995	−0.46
	3 Years	
Best	January 1995 through December 1997	12.74
Worst	August 1997 through July 2000	6.45

Source: Morningstar. Multiyear data provided are average annual performances.

As you can see in Table 7.21, the volatility of the bunker portfolio is the lowest of all the models. The scatter plot reflects this as well (see Figure 7.4). Every fund is in the sought-after northwest or upper left portion of the scatter plot. That means each of the funds should give a higher return with lower risk.

Table 7.21   Bunker Portfolio Standard Deviation versus S&P 500 through June 30, 2002

	3 Years		5 Years	
	Portfolio	*S&P 500*	*Portfolio*	*S&P 500*
Standard deviation	3.22	15.56	3.73	18.78

Source: Morningstar.

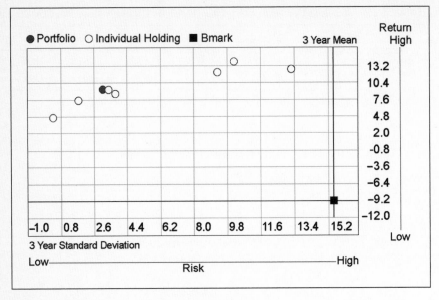

Figure 7.4   Bunker Portfolio Scatter Plot
Source: Morningstar.

Step 7, Know Your Team: Summing Up

So there you have it. Those are the four model portfolios. If you can, be-fore investing run your fund picks through similar historical tests. You won't be sorry. In case you want the numbers behind my current favorite funds, Table 7.22 includes some statistical data on the funds I used. Go ahead. Check them out. Then go on in the next chapter to read about some of my favorite managers. Just don't forget to keep doing your own homework, too. That's what counts over the long run.

Table 7.22 Fund Information Matrix

June Fund	YTD (%)	2001 (%)	2000 (%)	3-yr (%)	5-yr (%)	10-yr (%)	M-star Risk	M-star Return	Standard Deviation	Style	M-star Rating	Manager, Date
Equity Funds												
Calamos Growth	−3.82	−7.68	26.59	18.69	22.94	19.86	Average	High	45.01	Medium growth	5 Star	John Calamos 9/90
Clipper	−0.86	10.26	37.40	12.35	14.18	17.07	Below average	High	12.40	Large value	5 Star	James Gipson 2/84
First Eagle SoGen Global	9.95	10.21	9.72	13.56	9.35	11.54	Average	High	10.24	Medium value	5 Star	Jean-Marie Eveillard Charles de Vaulx 1/79
FMI Focus	−8.50	2.53	23.41	15.27	27.03	—	Average	High	32.41	Small growth	5 Star	Richard Lane 10/97
Growth Fund of America	−27.49	−12.28	7.49	−0.86	11.51	14.02	Average	High	22.39	Large growth	5 Star	Multiple 1/86
Hartford Midcap	−3.06	−4.65	24.86	8.95	—	—	Below average	High	26.99	Medium growth	5 Star	Phillip Perelmuter 12/97
Oakmark Fund	−4.54	18.29	11.78	0.60	5.34	15.34	High	High	18.21	Large value	4 Star	William Nygren 3/00
Oakmark Equity & Income	0.86	18.01	19.89	11.89	13.99	—	Average	High	9.34	Medium blend	5 Star	Clyde McGregor 11/95

(Continued)

Table 7.22 (Continued)

June Fund	YTD (%)	2001 (%)	2000 (%)	3yr (%)	5yr (%)	10yr (%)	M-star Risk	M-star Return	Standard Deviation	Style	M-star Rating	Manager, Date
Olstein Financial Alert	-4.37	17.25	12.93	10.04	18.28	—	High	High	25.12	Medium value	5 Star	Bob Olstein 9/95
Royce Low-Price Stock	-2.06	25.07	23.95	19.88	17.57	—	Above average	High	26.34	Small value	5 Star	George Whitney 12/99
Thornburg Value	-13.99	-8.11	3.96	-1.88	9.96	—	Average	High	15.72	Large blend	5 Star	William Fries 10/95
Bond Funds												
FPA New Income	5.79	12.33	9.32	9.08	7.81	8.14	Below average	Above average	3.52	Intermediate-term	4 Star	Robert Rodriguez 7/84
Harbor Bond	4.11	9.03	11.34	9.03	7.92	7.97	Average	High	3.90	Intermediate-term	5 Star	William Gross 12/87
SIT U.S. Gov. Secs.	3.01	8.44	9.08	7.26	6.67	6.45	Average	High	1.88	Short-term	5 Star	Michael Brilley 6/87
Vanguard Infl. Prot. Secs.	7.37	7.71	5.92	—	—	—	—	—	—	Short-term	—	Team 6/00
Indexes												
Lehman Bros. Agg. Bond	3.80	8.42	11.63	8.11	7.57	7.34						
MSCI EAFE	-10.60	-17.54	-8.46	-7.59	-1.01	5.11						
Russell 2000	-4.70	2.49	-3.03	1.67	4.44	10.96						
S&P 400 MidCap	-3.21	-0.60	17.49	6.66	12.57	15.05						
S&P 500	-13.15	-11.88	-9.10	-9.17	3.66	11.42						

Source: Morningstar. Multiyear data provided are average annual returns. All data through June 2002.

174

Chapter 8

Step 8: Get to Know the Players

You've heard a lot from me already about commitment to your investing strategy. Part of that dedication should include setting aside time to learn how the pros think. Whether you keep abreast of the trendsetters and theories through the Internet, the old-fashioned newspaper, or 24-hour cable newscasts, the important thing is that you do it.

I'll briefly discuss a few of my favorite managers in this chapter. In each case, I'll focus on one fund, although many of these managers quarterback more than that. (Returns provided are load-adjusted. Performance data was obtained from Morningstar, Inc.) I don't agree with everything these managers have to say, but I respect each of them and at one time have invested with them. I think we can all learn a lot from their experiences.

Rick Lane

Date of birth: December 22, 1955
Managing money since: 1981
Hobbies: Golf, skiing
Fund: FMI Focus (Symbol: FMIOX)
Morningstar investing style box: Small-cap blend

	One-Year	Five-Year	Since Inception
FMI Focus	–9.6%	14.0%	22.5%

All data are average annual returns through 9/30/02 and are provided by Morningstar. To obtain a prospectus for FMI Focus call 800-811-5311.

You won't find hard-core growth managers among my manager picks because I don't like managers who take unnecessary risks with my clients' money. Unfortunately, all too many growth managers do. When I allocate funds to fit the growth section of my clients' portfolios, I want someone who thinks intelligently about risk. Someone like Rick Lane. I like Rick because he takes calculated risks.

Rick is something of a freestyler. As you may recall, freestylers are some of my favorite kinds of managers because they don't get stuck in a category. They do their level best for their investors, whatever the market conditions. Freestyle managers can cause some confusion in your research. Exactly where do they fit in the portfolio allocation? At times it can be tough to tell. But ultimately, consistently good returns are what count.

Rick, who places himself in the small-cap blend category, uses value techniques to pick so-called growth stocks. Actually, he rejects the idea of any particular stock being a value or growth play. Instead, he says all stocks are cyclical. The key is to figure out which industries are poised to enter a growth cycle—and then buy the undervalued stocks in that industry.

He looks to buy a stock at a 25 to 30 percent discount to the price that the firm would fetch if bought by another company in its industry. Finally, he seeks out companies that occupy an important niche and that have consistent earnings and good management. To dig this information out, Rick likes nothing more than to hop on a plane and investigate a company up close. He talks with everyone from management to suppliers and customers.

Not all his stocks are winners, but he has learned that through diversification he can cushion his losses. Despite doing his best to analyze a company, Rick says, there's no stopping a management bent on defrauding investors. However, he looks to a wide array of holdings for defense should it happen.

FMI Focus holds a relatively large number of stocks, especially for a "focus" fund—nearly 100 at the end of 2001. In addition, as he felt stocks were becoming overvalued, Rick increased his cash holding. By the end of 2001, FMI Focus had 10.4 percent of its assets in cash. Rick's approach earned his fund an average risk rating from Morningstar on both a three- and five-year trailing basis through June 2002. Rick appreciates risk, he says, because he has a large amount of his own and his family's money in the fund. He also believes that it's important to be practical and sell a plummeting stock if you can't figure out why it's falling.

He credits his grandfather and father—both stockbrokers—for teaching him to follow his own path and avoid fads. "I try to be a contrarian but in an intelligent way," Rick says. Like I said, that's my kind of growth.

Bill Gross

Date of birth: April 13, 1944
Managing money since: 1971
Hobbies: Yoga, stamp collecting
Fund: Harbor Bond (Symbol: HABDX)
Morningstar investing style box: High-quality intermediate-term

	One-Year	Five-Year	10-Year
Harbor Bond	8.9%	8.0%	7.9%

All data are average annual returns through 9/30/02 and are provided by Morningstar.
To obtain a prospectus for Harbor Bond call 800-422-1050.

Arguably the most influential bond authority in the United States, Bill Gross isn't the sort of buttoned-down Wall Streeter that you might expect to lord over the staid world of coupon clippers. Dubbed the "Bond King" by *Fortune* magazine, he's a playfully cerebral man who practices

yoga and sometimes offers up his age in months. (He was 696 months old as of this writing.)

As legend has it, the young and mathematically oriented Bill first honed his money management skills at Vegas blackjack tables, where he spent six months turning $200 into $10,000. Later, after a tour of duty in Vietnam, Bill used his gambling proceeds to help pay for his MBA tuition at UCLA.[1]

"Basically, gambling and money management are pretty much the same," Bill says. In each, he explains, the goal is to spread the risk and avoid becoming emotional while staying focused on the odds.

Now, I can imagine that you're scratching your head at this, especially considering all my warnings against high-risk investments. Just how could a self-avowed gambler be one of my favorite managers?

The answer, as always, is in the performance. Bill has consistently and successfully played the odds. Bill is backed by a superior team of managers and analysts whose assessments of interest-rate direction and the overall global economy build a solid foundation for the funds' moves. Their work hasn't gone unnoticed. Bill and his team at Pimco were collectively named Morningstar's Fund Managers of the Year in both 1998 and 2000.

Bill's Harbor Bond fund, like many good fixed-income investments, has been an excellent hedge against bear markets. For example, while the S&P 500 plummeted 28.2 percent in 2002 through the end of the third quarter (September 30, 2002), Harbor Bond climbed 7.7 percent. Even in better markets, these funds are the types that offer investors a chance for the defense to score. I'd wager on Bill's odds of success.

Bob Rodriguez

Date of birth: December 13, 1948
Managing money since: 1974
Hobbies: Auto racing, watching movies with wife Sue
Fund: FPA New Income (Symbol: FPNIX)
Morningstar investing style box: High-quality short-term

	One-Year	Five-Year	10-Year
FPA New Income	0.2%	5.8%	7.0%

All data are average annual returns through 9/30/02 and are provided by Morningstar. To obtain a prospectus for FPA New Income call 800-982-4372.

Some people don't understand how a conservative value investor like Bob Rodriguez could feel at home in the high-octane world of auto racing. But it makes perfect sense to me. Bob, who loves racing with the Porsche Owners Club and the Porsche Club of America, also sees parallels between his hobby and his professional life. Both activities demand that risks and rewards are carefully balanced. The price of recklessness is just too high.

This skill is something Bob has clearly mastered and it is one of the reasons I have so much confidence in him. He takes some chances to get to the finish line, but he is always careful about minimizing downside risk. As a result, his FPA New Income fund has stayed the course over the long term.

Bob has been at the helm of the fund since 1984. Bob is also something of a Renaissance man—he deftly manages both bonds and stocks in another fund. His FPA New Income which, according to Morningstar, hasn't posted an annual loss since 1984, also earned Bob Morningstar's title of Fixed-Income Manager of the Year for 2001.

Bob's investing style is one that wins by not losing, Bob says. What does he mean by this? Typically between 55 percent and 70 percent of the fund's assets are invested in government and agency securities. When interest rates are low, Bob buys more bonds with shorter durations to avoid getting caught with overpriced bonds when interest rates rise. He does the opposite during periods of high interest rates. This approach has helped to reduce volatility and make the fund a solid long-term player.

While Bob's approach means his fund's return may lag other bond funds for a lap or two, he'll generally end up in the winner's circle. As we discussed, it's better to keep your eye on truly long-term performance than any one given year. Should a fund slide temporarily, ideally your diversified portfolio will help cushion you in the short term until the market swings back into your favor. So if you've found yourself a good manager who has proven himself or herself over the long haul, hang on for the ride. Let's just hope that manager's driving a Porsche.

Bob Olstein

Date of birth: July 7, 1941
Managing money since: 1980
Hobbies: Skiing, tuna fishing, golf, tennis
Fund: Olstein Financial Alert (Symbol: OFALX)
Morningstar investing style box: Mid-cap blend

	One-Year	Five-Year	Since Inception
Olstein Financial Alert	−9.4%	8.4%	14.5%

All data are average annual returns through 9/30/02 and are provided by Morningstar. To obtain a prospectus for Olstein Financial Alert call 800-799-2113.

Bob Olstein got badly burned back in 1968 when executives at a company he was analyzing exaggerated the health of their business. A rookie securities analyst on Wall Street, Bob took the executives' bait and made his first-ever stock recommendation.

"I thought my job was to go interview management and that they would not lie," Olstein recalls. "I lost a lot of money for people." But he also learned a valuable lesson. A colleague showed Bob how a closer examination of the balance sheet would have provided a heads-up on the problems. Bob has taken the advice to heart ever since. In the 1970s Bob went on to coauthor *The Quality of Earnings Report*, an influential newsletter dedicated to the premise that the quality of financial numbers matters. The report studied company financials and alerted readers to potential dangers.

Bob has put his nose for numbers to work as a money manager, too, eventually opening his own shop in 1995. Still true to his beliefs, he avoids the opportunities to speak with management that many other fund managers seek. "I'd rather spend the night with an annual report looking at what they're doing than going out and talking to them and interpreting what they are saying," says Bob.

What red flags does he look for? Numbers that smell funny, such as accounts receivable that are rising faster than sales, suggesting that future sales might be in jeopardy. A clean balance sheet is only the first hurdle a company must clear before it makes it onto Bob's buy list. He also wants a low price. He seeks companies that are trading at least 20 percent below their intrinsic value. When the stock reaches the target price, he sells, except when a reevaluation determines a higher price is merited. Bob firmly believes that selling is part of the key to winning, particularly in rocky times. "Anybody who has low turnover is at a big risk in these volatile markets because they're not capturing profits," says Bob.

Controlling risk is integral to long-term performance, Bob believes. "Long-term winners are the people who make the fewest mistakes." He reduces his risk by buying good stocks at bargain prices, and he doesn't bet the farm on any one stock. At any given time, Bob's portfolio may hold 100 stocks or more.

As for categorizing himself, Bob doesn't have a lot of patience for the fund "style" business. "Hogwash" is just about his view on it. Why? Because all funds want to buy stocks that grow, not just growth funds. And all funds want to buy stocks that have some kind of value, not just value investors. And all funds' performances should be compared to one another because every fund manager's job is to make money, he says.

"I'm an equity manager," says Bob. "I go across all disciplines and it's my job to make my clients money without taking a lot of risk." Olstein's multidisciplinarian approach is reflected by Morningstar's rating systems. In May 2002 Olstein Financial Alert was shifted into the mid-cap blend style box even though Morningstar still places the fund in the mid-cap value category. I consider Bob a freestyle manager, and he calls himself an eclectic value manager.

But before you tear up your game plan strategy and head for the beach on Bob's advice, you need to hear him out. He advises investors to invest their money with different successful managers who practice varied styles. He just prefers to think about the human beings behind the funds rather than the labels.

I really like Bob's insight and agree with him—to a point. I still believe that categories are valuable guides that investors do well to pay attention to. Use them as frames of reference to pick your funds. But if a fund you're considering doesn't fit snugly into a set allocation you're trying to fill, don't forget the big picture. Will the fund make you money in up and down markets? If the answer is yes, you want it. And that's where Bob's fund has filled the bill for many of my clients year in and year out.

Bob says he hopes to live to 100 and has no plans to retire. Even if he does, he's not a one-man band. Bob has a solid team helping him research and invest. So if you're thinking of putting your money in his fund, he's ready for the long haul. Just don't ask him about styles.

Bill Fries

Date of birth: February 22, 1939
Managing money since: 1979
Hobbies: Trout fishing, golf, reading
Fund: Thornburg Value (Symbol: TVAFX)
Morningstar investing style box: Large-cap blend

	One-Year	Five-Year	Since Inception
Thornburg Value	–24.0%	2.3%	10.6%

All data are average annual returns through 9/30/02 and are provided by Morningstar.
To obtain a prospectus for Thornburg Value call 800-847-0200.

Bill Fries is hard to classify. Despite its name, his Thornburg Value fund sits in Morningstar's large-cap blend fund category. As I said in Chapter 4, Bill Fries is one of my favorite managers—a top-notch freestyler.

How does Bill define his style? He doesn't object to the blend category. But more specifically, Bill is looking for something he calls "comprehensive value" rather than classical value. He borrows from the value investor's approach by mostly purchasing stocks selling at low price-to-

earnings ratios and at valuations that are beneath the underlying business' expected growth rate.

But he also considers companies with consistent earnings as well as those that he calls "emerging franchises." These are businesses in the early stage of their development with a commanding role in their industry and pricing power to boot. Because the performance of this last category of stock is less predictable, Bill controls risk by limiting this group to account for less than 25 percent of his total portfolio. In the volatile market of late 2002, that percentage was trimmed back to about 15 percent.

If there's one main difference between Bill and his strict value colleagues, it's that Bill doesn't think the balance sheet numbers that traditional value investors rely on tell a company's whole story. "I do not believe they capture all of what is valuable in a stock," Bill says. "They don't even come close."

Bill values qualities that are not quantifiable, such as an honest corporate culture and candid management. "When I find there's a reluctance to answer questions that are reasonable and I know that management knows that information, that sends up a red flag for me," Bill says. He has walked away from a number of companies after an unsatisfying interview. The accounting scandals that rocked the market in 2002 made very clear the dramatic impact that these so-called intangibles can have.

And when does he sell? In the case of true value stocks, he waits until they hit his predetermined target price for an 18-to-20-month period. In the case of stocks that are developing new franchises, Bill is less rigid. He might reevaluate his target price and, if he decides the valuation has increased, hold the stock for another year or so.

But the outcome is not always rosy. Sometimes the sales are a matter of pure risk control. This happens when stocks continue to fall away from the initial target prices set by Bill, or when he's decided the reward of a new stock has more potential than any one of his existing holdings.

Bill, who has over half of his personal investment money in his own funds, said the volatile 2002 market posed the biggest challenge of his career to his goal of consistency. "There are lots of reasons why someone could be persuaded to become extremely defensive and have a portfolio that was not diversified to include media and tech stocks," says Bill, who had a tough year in 2002. "But I'm not sure that works forever."

Bill attributes some of his independent outlook to his location in New Mexico, nearly 2,000 miles from Wall Street. "There's not a crowd of investment people in Santa Fe," he says. His outlook, he says, is informed by the ideas of real people.

Bill Nygren

Date of birth: 1958
Managing money since: 1996
Hobbies: Softball, sports fan
Fund: Oakmark (Symbol: OAKMX)
Morningstar investing style box: Large-cap blend

	One-Year	Five-Year	10-Year
Oakmark	−11.8%	0.4%	12.2%

All data are average annual returns through 9/30/02 and are provided by Morningstar. To obtain a prospectus for Oakmark call 800-625-6275.

As we discussed in Chapter 5, the difference between one value manager and another can be huge—even within a given fund family. Consider Bill Nygren. Bill has been in the investment industry since 1981 and has been managing money since 1996. He was tapped to manage the Oakmark fund after his predecessor Robert Sanborn stumbled in 1998 and 1999. (Bill cut his teeth managing another Oakmark fund but at press time Oakmark is the only one open to new investors.) By the end of 2000 and Bill's first year, the fund under Bill had pulled back into the black, posting an 11.8 percent return that trounced the S&P 500 by 20.9 percentage points. He did it again in 2001 with an 18.3 percent return, a 22.8 percentage point improvement over the benchmark index.

The mutual fund press has written a good deal about Bob Sanborn's so-called deep-value style and Bill's less traditional value approach. But Bob's successor downplays the style differences. "I think of both Robert and myself as pure value investors," Bill says, though his fund's less traditional approach to value is reflected in its "blend" position in the Morningstar style box.

Where does Bill see himself on the value spectrum? He says his methodology for determining whether to buy a stock is less traditional than the criteria he uses for selling stocks. On the buy side, Bill likes to pick stocks that are priced at 60 percent of what the company would be worth to an outside buyer. He also looks for companies with good growth prospects and that have a management with a demonstrated history of success. Bill especially likes executives who own stock in their companies.

Bill's buying decisions are much more old school than his selling decisions, which are more formula-driven. If all goes as planned, Bill sells stocks once they climb to within 90 percent of their intrinsic value. "We are very disciplined quantitatively on the sell side," he says.

While Bill's methods for picking stocks may have remained the same over time, the names and types of stocks in his funds have not. By the second half of 2002, his portfolios had companies with slightly higher growth potential and much higher capitalizations than he owned two years earlier. "Some people look at that and say, 'Wow, you're changing,'" Bill says. "I say, no, we're not changing at all. The opportunities that the market is creating have changed."

Jean-Marie Eveillard

Date of birth: January 23, 1940
Managing money since: 1979
Hobbies: Opera fan
Fund: First Eagle SoGen Global (Symbol: SGENX)
Morningstar investing style box: Mid-cap blend

	One-Year	Five-Year	10-Year
First Eagle SoGen Global	5.9%	5.6%	9.8%

All data are average annual returns through 9/30/02 and are provided by Morningstar. To obtain a prospectus for First Eagle SoGen Global call 800-334-2143.

Jean-Marie Eveillard divides investors into two basic camps. There are those who think they know what will happen in the future and those who know they don't. Jean-Marie, a value manager, places himself squarely among the unknowing. "The future belongs to God," Jean-Marie says. "And he ain't telling."

Because of this uncertainty, Jean-Marie has long been interested in stable but sometimes unexciting businesses. He also finds the predictable yields of bonds to be appealing and has always valued gold as a kind of insurance policy. Before buying a stock in a company, Jean-Marie analyzes the business to figure out what a knowledgeable buyer would pay in an all-cash acquisition of the entire company. He will buy a stock if it is trading at a discount of anywhere from 5 to 50 percent below that price. The smaller discounts are unusual and warranted only in exceptional cases. More typically, Jean-Marie buys at a steep discount and sells holdings when the stock gets within 10 or even 20 percent of the intrinsic value he has determined it holds.

Grounded in the classic investment styles of Ben Graham and War-

ren Buffett, Jean-Marie has remained true to his investment philosophy in bull and bear times. While he may underperform in hypergrowth periods, his performance has been steady over time. What did Jean-Marie do differently in the good and bad markets? Nothing, he maintains. Whatever the economic environment, he continues to invest in undervalued stocks that fly below the radar of other investors seeking glamour.

He hasn't ventured into technology companies until recently because he felt they were overvalued and that their industries were changing too fast to be predictable. "We didn't own any new economy stocks on the way up and we didn't own them on the way down." The defensive approach has drawn criticism. In the middle of 1988, Jean-Marie pulled the predecessor fund to First Eagle SoGen Global out of the Tokyo stock market because he felt that market was overinflated and headed for a downturn. But for a while after he made the move that market continued to rise, and Jean-Marie recalls one critic who observed that he owned "zip in the second-largest equity market in the world." Jean-Marie was later vindicated when the market crashed.

Jean-Marie plans to retire in 2005 and expects his funds will make a smooth transition to a new regime. For one, Jean-Marie says, he has committed to leaving much of his investment stakes in the funds for several years. Also, Charles de Vaulx, comanager of the First Eagle So-Gen Global fund, has been working with Jean-Marie for about 15 years, and Jean-Marie expects his colleague's continued presence will offer great consistency. While Charles has not officially been tapped to take the top manager spot, Jean-Marie believes it is a likely scenario. Says Jean-Marie: "The investment approach will not change."

Step 8, Get to Know the Players: Summing Up

The market is about more than numbers. It's important to take time to learn and understand the people behind the numbers (and your returns). The process can help you learn to pick the managers and funds that will pave the way to your financial goals.

Chapter 9

Step 9: How Ya Doin'?

When Ed Koch was mayor of New York City back in the late 1970s and 1980s, he was constantly asking, "How am I doing?" He didn't always get the answers he wanted. But that didn't stop him from asking. I think the practice made him a better mayor and provided the awareness he needed to help stabilize the Big Apple financially.

Keeping a tally of your progress toward financial goals doesn't come so naturally to most people. I see a wide range of approaches when I meet potential clients for the first time. Some know exactly where they are and explain point by point where they stand. But most are only vaguely aware of their situation. "We're down a lot!" they'll say. Or, "We're doing okay."

Unfortunately, bear markets like the one in 2000–2002 compound the problem. Investors who got a kick in boom times logging onto the Internet to watch their money grow lost the will to keep tabs on their shrinking finances. As the market scraped along the bottom, some people didn't even open their monthly statements anymore. I don't blame them. It's not much fun to check in when you're losing. But checking in is the only way to know if you're meeting your investing goals.

The purpose of this chapter is to encourage you to adopt Mayor Koch's attitude—no matter what the market looks like. Think back for a minute to the three C's emphasized in Chapter 1. You now have a *commitment* to an investing game plan. You are *consistently* making the right plays regarding your goals, your risk tolerance, and the allocation that helped you set up a diversified portfolio.

Here is where the *courage* comes in. You need the courage to identify where your portfolio stands. You need to confront any problems. Then you need to take any necessary action to keep your game plan on track. Sometimes that simply means staying the course.

The other C's come into play here, too. You need to make a commitment to monitoring your portfolio. You need to monitor it consistently. Ultimately that monitoring will require you to have the courage to make decisions—to hold steady or to shift course.

To find out how you're doing, I suggest do-it-yourselfers adopt a three-step process that I've developed over the years. If you are working with an advisor you should expect him or her to go through a similar set of reviews and periodically apprise you of the results. Either way, I assure you that you'll always be able to answer Ed Koch's question. More importantly, you're more likely to achieve your financial goals. The process entails:

1. *Tactical Assessments.* Develop a twice-monthly system to monitor the underlying investments (funds) that are driving your game plan.

Hayden Play:
Keep score.

The investment industry wants nothing more than for you to fork over your money and forget about it. But contrary to the blind buy-and-hold mantra, you should stay abreast of your investments. Knowing where your money is invested and how it's doing will help you make better decisions, not worse. Do-it-yourselfers should tally the progress of their investments twice a month (I check in on 421 funds every Friday). If you're working with an advisor you're not off the hook—you'll need to make sure he or she has a good system to track your progress and apprise you of developments. Just don't let the near-term focus make you lose track of your long-term strategy.

2. *Strategic Reviews.* Annually or (even better) semiannually evaluate your investment strategy as well as your personal financial needs.

3. *Action (Just Do It!).* After taking the time to consider the information you've gathered, decide whether action is called for. Then do it—change your allocation and/or strategy when necessary.

Even a game plan headed for a loss can be rerouted. But you need to stay informed to be ready to act.

Getting the Routine Down: Tactical Assessments

This first step is primarily for do-it-yourselfers. Why? If you are one, it's your responsibility to monitor on a regular basis how your underlying investments are doing. If you have an advisor or planner, you should discuss his or her approach to ongoing monitoring of your funds. Then if you are satisfied with the system, you're set. Delegating this task is generally one of the reasons people hire advisors in the first place.

By contrast, if you are on your own, you've got to think of yourself like a coach who evaluates the effectiveness of not only each play but each player as well. Likewise, you have to determine whether each fund is performing the way it is supposed to.

How often to check in? Although this is somewhat subjective, I'd advise you to evaluate each fund no more often than twice monthly. Many managers and advisors, myself included, monitor funds more frequently, and that's fine. However, I don't advise do-it-yourselfers to watch the funds that closely because it is too tempting to make changes, and that would distort your longer-term strategy. I have seen too many people overfocus at this level as a result of too-frequent monitoring. If you make changes too often at the tactical level in reaction to a short-term event in the market, you will inevitably block the effectiveness of your overall game plan.

What information should you look for, and where can you find it? Unfortunately, monthly or quarterly statements provided by brokerage houses or fund firms typically report only the value of the investment in a given fund. That doesn't tell you much about how the fund is doing. It is almost impossible to know where you're at in your game plan if you cannot evaluate performance of a fund in comparison to the market benchmarks and other funds in its style category. To get this information, you'll need to do some basic (and relatively easy) legwork on your own.

You want to know how each fund has performed on a year-to-date basis, as expressed by the percentage change in value for that time period. (If it's very early in the year, consider comparing to other like funds by looking at the trailing one-year returns.) You also want to be aware of how each fund is performing in comparison to other top funds in its fund style. As we've discussed earlier, this information is available in most newspapers (*Investor's Business Daily*, the *Wall Street Journal*, *Barron's*, or the *New York Times*) or online on many financial web sites (www.morningstar.com and http://finance.yahoo.com).

What kinds of changes in fund performance should you be concerned about? Typically, a red flag goes up for me when I see a fund that is doing 10 percentage points worse than other top-performing funds in the same style. For instance, if the best large-cap value funds are down 5 percent from the beginning of a year and the large-cap value fund I am using is down about 15 percent, I know the manager must be having a problem.

Now that doesn't mean I drop that fund right then and there. As any good coach will tell you, you have to give plays time to develop. Applying that concept to mutual funds means that you need to have some patience. Good managers will run into rough patches from which it may take them as long as a year to recover. You have to be careful to differentiate between a manager who is temporarily underperforming and one who has lost his or her ability to perform on a longer-term basis.

Deciding the difference between these two situations is very difficult. Your twice-monthly tracking may give you a heads-up on a problem. You can also get information by reading the financial press' coverage of your funds, as we discussed in Chapter 6. Additionally, if you have questions about your fund you can't answer, you can call and discuss concerns with your mutual fund sales representative.

If you're still concerned about the fund, it may be time to sell. While there are no hard-and-fast rules when it comes to deciding to dump a fund, there are two triggers that generally guide me to sell. Ideally, it is an action not done lightly or quickly but an informed judgment call made after watching a fund's performance over a 6-to-12-month period.

The first sell trigger is when it becomes apparent that you are obviously uncomfortable with the degree of risk of a particular fund. This may not be obvious at first. For example, during the bull market you may have been invested in one of the many funds that were technology-heavy. As your fund dropped and rebounded like a yo-yo, you weren't sure what to do. On the days it rose, you felt better. When it fell, you felt sick and couldn't sleep. When a fund's volatility begins to affect how you feel, it's time to sell.

The second trigger is a quantitative measure. Remember I said that a red flag goes up for me when a fund underperforms by 10 percentage points in comparison to the top funds in its style? Well, if that fund continues to slide and is down 15 to 20 percentage points more than the best funds in its style on a year-to-date basis, it's generally time to sell. There may be serious issues that call for getting out of the fund.

In addition to the short-term monitoring, your tactical assessment should also include an overall performance report for your total portfolio. I suggest you do this on a quarterly basis. What should you track? You should consider how much money you started investing with originally as well as what you started and ended with in the period you're monitoring. It should also show what percentage gain or loss you've had in your portfolio over that term. A sample of the type of report you might ideally use is shown in Table 9.1. This is a streamlined version of the report I give my clients every quarter.

In summary, both the twice-monthly tracking of your funds and the quarterly monitoring of your portfolio will help you keep abreast of how your funds are doing on a tactical basis.

While this is a challenging task, it can act as an early warning system for problems that might be developing. Just don't react too quickly to downswings. Carefully evaluate the fund's situation as well as the overall sector and market.

Table 9.1   Quarterly Performance Report

Beginning Portfolio Value on March 31, 2002	$_____
Additions	$_____
Withdrawals	$_____
Ending Portfolio Value June 30, 2002	$_____
Net or original amount invested (principal)	$_____
Gain/loss from net amount invested (principal)	$_____
% Return for both quarter and trailing 12 months	_____%

The reason for short-term tracking is to make sure the mechanisms (funds) that ultimately work together to achieve your long-term plans are not getting derailed. Think of the process as you would the checks and repairs that engineers routinely make on a train starting a cross-country trip. For safety's sake, the trains have to be consistently checked, and sometimes the moving parts have to be replaced at various station stops along the way. But the overall journey goes on.

Now that you have an idea how the monitoring and tracking of your funds work, let's talk about the broader subject of reviewing your game plan.

Strategic Reviews

The second step in your evaluation process is a broad-based strategic review of your overall allocation strategy and goal(s). This should be done at least once a year. It's often easiest to do in January as you prepare your taxes because you'll have the previous year's data to look over. But pick any date that works for you. Your birthday, the start of the school year, or summertime when your business is slow. Just be consistent: Pick it and stick with it!

There are two parts to this element of the process. First, you need to check in and determine whether the overall investment game plan is still sound. Second, you need to determine whether any changes in your personal situation necessitate a change in your strategy. Use these two checklists to evaluate your overall investment game plan and personal situation.

Investment Checklist

- Is the plan meeting your goal of a certain return rate? (You established your return rate when developing your goals in Chapter 3.) For your overall portfolio, meeting your return rate is more important than a comparison to any one benchmark.
- Is the allocation between stocks, bonds, and cash still appropriate given your tolerance for risk? Has it felt too risky, not risky enough, or just about right? If it was too risky you may trim back the offense and add a bit to the defense. Or, if not risky enough, you can do the opposite and increase the offense. Do you feel you need to take the risk test again?
- Are your portfolio's allocation levels to the various asset classes and fund styles still appropriate given the market conditions? For example, when growth funds became overvalued in 1999, you might have wanted to decrease the percentage you had invested in growth and increase your allocation to value funds. You might make changes like these through the year, but this strategic review process assures that you will check out allocation levels at least once a year.
- Do you need to trim back or add to your investments in any of the funds in order to make your fund styles and asset classes match your strategy?
- Is the inflation rate you assumed in your planning still valid?

Personal Checklist

Some changes in the structure of your personal life can require you to adjust your game plan. You need to determine whether the assumptions about your life that you used to create your original plan remain intact. Here are a few issues to keep in mind:

- Has the date you expect to retire remained unchanged?
- If you're not retired yet, review your retirement goal. Has anything changed that will affect the annual income you'll need at retirement?
- Has the amount of money you assumed you could invest each year changed?
- Did you have any personal losses or gains (such as in a business or a death) over the period that could affect your planning?
- Do you have enough money in reserve for emergencies and contingencies?
- Did you discover anything new about yourself that could affect your game plan?

Time Out to Consider Rebalancing

Any action you take affects your overall game plan. Some planners think you should tweak your portfolio to stay loyal to the precise contours of your original game plan. In the jargon of the business, it's called rebalancing. This is a concept that is the subject of much debate in the industry. Rebalancing means that you react to one asset class growing and another shrinking by acting to maintain your original allocation percentages.

As a general rule, I think rebalancing is a good idea. It forces you to sell high (the asset that has moved up the most to cause the imbalance) and buy low (the asset that is out of favor and cheaper at this time). Imagine if you had done that at the end of 1999 when there were outsized gains in many stocks. You would have trimmed back to your original stock allocation by selling at a high and investing in bond funds going into the year 2000. Rebalancing at that time would have put you in much better shape to withstand the impending crash.

Now let's look at a hypothetical portfolio and consider whether rebalancing makes sense. Let's assume you started out one year ago with the allocation shown in Table 9.2. After a triumphant year in equities your portfolio's allocation shifted as shown in Table 9.3.

Should you sell 10 percent of the stock funds and use the proceeds to add to the bond funds to restore the portfolio to its original 60-35-5 percent allocation? Although it may not be the right decision in all cases, I would generally say yes.

Why? Rebalancing generally lowers risk and at times can increase returns. Other times it may lower returns. If you had rebalanced every year during the 1995 to 2000 run-up you might not have gained as much, but during 2000 through 2002, you would have lost much less.

However, I don't advise that you be a slave to rebalancing. The beauty of active asset allocation is that it lets you take into account market shifts. An aggressive portfolio might have seemed perfect in the late 1990s, but by 2002 you've understandably grown more risk averse. If you sense that you've outgrown your allocation strategy, it doesn't make sense to keep following it. Likewise, if you've made a decision to be more opportunistic on the fringes of your portfolio, I'm not averse to letting some of the winners run.

What's important is that you take some time to consider the question of rebalancing in the ever-changing market. You can do this after doing your broad semiannual or annual review. Or you can continually monitor your allocation's percentage levels. For example, you could decide to rebalance anytime an asset class is 10 to 15 percentage points over or under the original allocation. What I generally do is consider rebalancing whenever an asset class is 15 percentage points over the original allocation or every year, whichever comes sooner. Of course if I'm shifting strategies I won't rebalance.

Table 9.2 One Year Ago	
Stock funds	60%
Bond funds	35%
Cash equivalents	5%

Table 9.3 After a Triumphant Year	
Stock funds	70%
Bond funds	25%
Cash equivalents	5%

Just Do It!

Okay, you say, you've been given a lot of homework. How do you make sure you get it all done and keep it straight? An old-fashioned to-do list will keep you efficient. Consider creating one similar to the list shown in Table 9.4. This step evolves out of your frequent monitoring and broad reviewing. As you monitor your funds, performance reports, and checklists, you'll notice various changes that may trigger you to act.

Pull your to-do list out each time you do your tactical (fund level) assessment as well as the annual or semiannual strategic (overall game

Table 9.4   The Action List

Item	Date to Complete	By Whom
Tactical Level		
1. Sell X fund (manager change).	April 18	Me/advisor
2. Buy Y fund (fill vacancy on offense).	May 3	Me/advisor
3. _____	_____	_____
4. _____	_____	_____
Strategic Level		
1. Rebalance allocation.	January 5	Me/advisor
2. Sell shares of the following funds for rebalancing: _____	January 5	Me/advisor
3. Buy shares of the following funds for rebalancing: _____	January 5	Me/advisor
4. Shift 10% from growth style to value style. Sell the following funds:	February 1	Me/advisor
Buy the following funds:		
5. Add $10,000 more to my investments.	November 1	Me
6. Summarize actions in writing.	November 15	Me

plan) review. Write down any actions you want to take with a deadline. Then revisit the list every other week when you do your monitoring to make sure you've taken the action you planned. This will help assure that what you want to get done actually gets done.

When you've taken action, your work is not done. You've got to document it so that you know not only where your investing game plan stands but where your tax situation stands as well. Create a file in your filing cabinet or computer to hold brief memoranda that summarize any changes you've made.

Step 9, How Ya Doin'?: Summing Up

If you design yourself a way to review your game plan status you will never get too far off course. Even if you have an advisor, you may want to discuss his or her review process. Though there are variations, a review discipline should include shorter-term tactical monitoring and less frequent strategic reviews and action. The process will help you stay well informed and aware of where you stand with regard to your investing game plan. Oh yes, and you'll make Ed Koch proud.

Chapter 10

Step 10: Write It Up!

By now you know I'm a firm believer in plans. In Steps 1 through 9 I've outlined how to get, create, and work an investing game plan. But there's one final step I urge you to take, one last tool for your investing arsenal.

This last one will bolster the commitment, consistency, and courage it takes to wade through the process. No, it's not some fancy software. Rather, it's the incredible power of the written word. Over the years, I've witnessed the profound effect that a single investing game plan document can have on investors' discipline levels.

Setting down goals, objectives, and how you plan to arrive at them in black and white helps bring any questions to light before they become problems. Perhaps most importantly, doing so can solidify your resolve.

What is such a document comprised of? Just as all game plans are different, so too do formal summaries vary. They needn't be complex. The best of them simply state the goals and benchmarks that were set and the thought process that led you to establish them. When I write game plans up for clients I provide an outline of the assumptions we've made and the goals we hope for. (I also include some language outlining my firm's responsibilities and views, something do-it-yourselfers will not need to address.)

If you're working with an advisor or a brokerage firm, you may be given more formal summaries than the hypothetical one I provide here. Study the document. Ask questions. A good advisor or planner will be happy to answer them. You may be uncertain of some of the wording. If there's too much jargon, rewrite it for yourself in plain English. You're the one who has to follow it.

Here is a sample of a game plan that I wrote for Robert, the hypothetical client whose retirement goal we discussed back in Chapter 3. I've inserted subheads throughout the plan to reflect the steps we've discussed in the book.

Investing Game Plan for
Mr. Robert Smith

Purpose
(Step 1: Get the Game Plan Mind-Set)

The purpose of your investing game plan is to outline the general framework that will govern how the assets in your account will be invested. The plan will help you attain your stated goals and objectives while taking into account your risk tolerance level and your unique needs.

We understand that you, Robert Smith, are developing your investing game plan so that in 20 years you will have the money you'll need to retire. We will invest money in the interim with the intention that, once retired, you can live off your withdrawals without depleting your principal.

This statement is not a contract and should not be constituted as any guarantee that your goal will be achieved. It is a formal declaration of our dual commitment to achieving your financial goals. As your planner I agree to adhere to the guidelines, investing methods, and strategy outlined below. As the investor, you agree to remain committed to consistent investing over time.

As your advisor we:

- Will help you achieve your personal benchmark as determined by your goals and ability to handle risk.
- Won't speculate or gamble with your money. The number-one rule in long-term investing is to *avoid serious losses.*

- Will allocate your money to various agreed-upon levels of fund asset classes and styles. The mix will ultimately determine your portfolio's long-term performance.

I believe that as a committed investor you are in the best position to succeed if you:

- Make the final decisions after getting the information you need from us and other relevant sources in order to make the best possible choices.
- Invest only in mutual funds—the instant diversification and liquidity they provide is unparalleled.

Market Volatility and Your Game Plan (Step 2: Know Your Risk Tolerance)

Our primary objective in managing your money is to help you reach your investment goals. To do that, the crucial factor that we look at is not how to manage rates of return, but how to manage the risk you take in the market.

You could potentially experience great anxiety over sudden losses in portfolio value like the kind many experienced in the Great Bear Market of 2000–2002. From January 2000 through June 2002, the S&P 500 Index plummeted 30.4 percent. This volatility—though disappointing to live through—is what investors have learned can happen in the market. While extreme, given recent history, it is what one needs to be prepared for. That knowledge may not help you stomach the awful losses of a bear market. It does, however, underscore the need to design a portfolio that reflects your tolerance for the market's short-term unpredictability.

If your portfolio is not properly calibrated to your risk tolerance, your portfolio might experience drastic changes in valuation due to volatility in the general market for which you're unprepared. This could lead you to attempt to recover your losses by making sudden and harmful changes to your portfolio. To help protect you from inevitable market swings, we need to first assess your risk level. It's important to:

- Decide what level of market risk it will take to reach your investment objectives. (Robert, you'll need to aim for an 8 percent annual return, the higher range of the rate that you could possibly get from a moderate portfolio.)
- Determine whether there is a difference between the risk required to meet your investment objectives and the degree of your personal risk tolerance. (You scored 12 on the Risk Quiz, the high end of risk steady, so the 8 percent return would be appropriate.)
- Create an investment portfolio that is consistent with your personal risk tolerance. (We'll create a portfolio with a moderate level of risk.)

Your Goal and Personal Benchmark
(Step 3: Know Your Goals)

After several meetings, we have mutually agreed on your goal. You aim to have a lump sum of $383,618 after 20 years. To get there, we'll begin by investing $651.28 monthly, though we'll review these figures each year.

Your personal benchmark is an annual growth rate of 8 percent annually. It is against this number that you will measure the progress of your game plan toward your goal. There is no standardized benchmark to which you can compare your whole portfolio with absolute precision.

At least twice a year we will meet to discuss the progress being made toward your objectives. This will also help to determine if you would like to be more aggressive or conservative as your portfolio becomes seasoned.

Portfolio Theory
(Step 4: Get the Fund Fever)

It is important to understand that your portfolio will be composed of a number of different mutual funds. The whole portfolio is the sum of the parts, but the most important issue is the interaction of those parts.

I believe one of the best ways to achieve your investing goal and control risk in your portfolio is by allocating your investments to achieve diversification. This is done in several ways. You will invest only in mutual funds because they offer more diversification than each individual underlying security itself. In addition, by allocating your money to a varied mix of fund investments you will diversify your portfolio.

The allocation process is comprised of three levels. They include choosing a varied mix of funds that hold different asset classes, that is, stocks, bonds, or cash (first level); selecting different styles, that is, size and type of stock and bond funds (second level); and investing in specific funds (third level).

Your Allocation
(Step 5: Get an Offense and a Defense)

From our previous discussions, our perception is that you want to take medium risk to achieve reasonable growth of your investment relative to the market. You are not looking for income from this portfolio for at least the next 20 years.

Your portfolio, designed to achieve an 8 percent annual return rate, is allocated as illustrated in Table 10.1. [Note: Readers, here you will recognize the allocation as the model moderate portfolio outlined in Chapter 5.] Of course, you should know that you are not likely to achieve exactly 8 percent annually, but we hope that over time the average annual return will be in the ballpark.

Table 10.1 **Robert Smith's Offense and Defense (First Level of Allocation)**

Equities	65%	(Offense)
Fixed income	25%	(Defense)
Cash	10%	(Defense)

As you can see, the majority of your investment will go to offense because you have sufficient time to cushion any volatility in the equity market. I am aware of your interest in the volatile telecom sector; we will do some research to determine whether we would advise you to invest in related sector funds. At this time we suggest you hold off from sectors, and at no time should more than 10 percent of your portfolio be in sectors.

We then go to the second level of allocation decisions and choose specific styles of stock funds and then bond funds (see Tables 10.2 and 10.3).

Table 10.2   Robert Smith's Stock Fund Style Mix (Second Level of Allocation)

	Value	Blend	Growth	Total
Large-cap	10%	10%	0%	20%
Medium-cap	20%	0%	10%	30%
Small-cap	7.5%	0%	7.5%	15%
Total	37.5%	10%	17.5%	65%

Table 10.3 Robert Smith's Bond Fund Style Mix (Second Level of Allocation)

	Short-Term	Intermediate-Term	Long-Term	Total
High-quality	10%	15%	0%	25%
Medium-quality	0%	0%	0%	0%
Low-quality	0%	0%	0%	0%
Total	10%	15%	0%	25%

Selecting Investments
(Steps 6 to 8: Pick and Know Your Players and Team)

Steps 6 through 8 constitute the nuts and bolts of picking specific funds. Together they make up the third and final level of allocation. We have analyzed thousands of mutual funds in hopes of finding superior managers. Our selection process looks at both quantitative and qualitative issues. We consider historical individual fund and portfolio performances and keep abreast of manager styles on an ongoing basis.

The funds must meet our criteria on their own and together as a unit. Of the great variety of measures that we use to gauge funds, past performance is one of the most important. Ideally a fund's performance should have met or exceeded the performance of the appropriate benchmark for its style for two out of three years and three years cumulatively, and for three out of five years and five years cumulatively (Step 6: Pick the Players).

Before investing we also tested your funds as a unit (Step 7: Know Your Team). We did this by analyzing the total portfolio's historical performance. We were satisfied that the risk level was appropriate. Among the data we considered was the fact that there were no negative returns over the trailing average annual return in the one-year, three-year, five-year, or ten-year term periods as calculated through June 30, 2002.

When researching managers (Step 8: Get to Know the Players), it's important to learn about their investment philosophies. They are generally identified as focusing on value or growth styles, or a blend of the two. They also specialize in investing in large, medium, or small companies. We prefer experienced managers who are consistent in their performance as well as their style.

After our reviews, we chose the funds outlined in Tables 10.4 and 10.5 for your portfolio and achieved the third level of allocation.

Periodic Adjustments
(Step 9: How Ya Doin'?)

We will monitor the performance of your funds on a twice-monthly basis. We will also provide you with an overall performance report on a quarterly basis. Among the details we'll provide are the amount of money you started investing with originally and how much you ended up with during any given period. Additionally, we will sit down with you at least semiannually to provide a strategic review of your game plan and discuss whether any adjustments are necessary.

As a result of the ongoing reviews, we may also suggest changing funds from time to time. Reasons may include market criteria that we

Table 10.4   Moderate Model/Stock Funds 65 Percent (Third Level of Allocation)

	Value	Blend	Growth	Total
Large-cap	Clipper 5% Oakmark 5%	Thornburg Value 10%	0%	20%
Medium-cap	Olstein Financial Alert 10% First Eagle SoGen Global 10%	0%	Hartford Midcap 10%	30%
Small-cap	Royce Low Price Stock 7.5%	0%	FMI Focus 7.5%	15%
Total	37.5%	10%	17.5%	65%

cannot control, such as new tax laws or economic shifts like changes in interest rates. Other factors within funds may also cause us to advise changes such as a manager's departure or a streak of poor stock picks.

At least once a year, we also will consider rebalancing your portfolio. We will not automatically do it, as changes in market conditions or your personal life may indicate that it's not appropriate to rebalance to return to our original allocation. If all conditions remain the same we

Table 10.5 Moderate Model/Fixed Income 25 Percent (Third Level of Allocation)

	Short-Term	*Intermediate-Term*	*Long-Term*	*Total*
High-quality	SIT U.S. Gov. Secs. 5% Vanguard Infl. Prot. Secs. 5%	FPA New Income 7.5% Harbor Bond 7.5%	0%	25%
Medium-quality	0%	0%	0%	0%
Low-quality	0%	0%	0%	0%
Total	10%	15%	0%	25%

could rebalance sooner than one year if the asset allocation percentages have changed by 15 percentage points or more (either up or down) from our original plan.

The Investing Game Plan
(Step 10: Write It Up!)

You've now created and have begun to work your investing game plan. This written statement is designed to formalize the process and act as a guide over the coming years as you continue toward your goal.

Step 10, Write It Up!: Summing Up

Just how successful you will be in winning your game plan will depend to a large extent on your ability to remain committed, consistent, and courageous in the face of market forces that are unpredictable over the short term. This written game plan is designed to strengthen your resolve. Now it's time to start working the game plan. That's the best—and only—route to winning it.

Chapter 11

SOS! Finding an Advisor

Now that we've reviewed the 10 steps to creating an investment game plan, you may feel ready to manage your own plan. You may believe you have the three T's to make it work: the time, the talent, and the temperament. It's a tough combination of criteria. But if you have them and you want to manage your plan on your own, I sincerely hope this book will help you do your job successfully.

What if you feel otherwise? You're concerned that in fact you don't have one of those T's. You believe you need a financial advisor to manage your plan for you.

This chapter is written for people:

- Who don't have the time to manage their game plans.
- Who don't have enough interest in the market to give their plans the attention they deserve.
- Whose temperament might not yield the best results.
- Who want to find a good investment advisor.

Perhaps one day not too long ago you thought you could manage your own plan. But lately you've started to have doubts. That's perfectly legitimate and understandable. The investing period since the mid 1990s has been the most unusual and challenging in our lifetimes. From 1995 through February of 2000 we had hypergrowth. A very seductive period, it made most people think it was easy to make money in the market. A monkey threw darts at a list of Nasdaq stocks and made over 100 percent in 1999. Professional money managers with disciplined long-term approaches to the stock market were scoffed at as Neanderthals who did not understand the new economy. Suggest bonds and the reply was "Get real!"

Then it happened. On March 10, 2000, the Nasdaq started its free fall. High-flying tech stocks started to crack. Within two months the telephone calls started coming in from people pleading for help. As the downturn unfolded, lifetime savings were left in ruins, marriages collapsed, and businesses went under.

The corruption emerged. We learned how top executives at companies failed their shareholders and employees. We learned that some brokerage houses and investment banks deceived the public. Onetime do-it-yourselfers felt not only that the market was hard to beat, but that the game was rigged to begin with.

Yet, there are still savings to be made, goals to be met. The question is how to do it while protecting yourself—your principal, your family's wealth.

That's where an advisor can help. An advisor is someone who helps you create, manage, and monitor your plan. In the age of mistrust, rampant greed, and the worst market since the Great Depression, even choosing an advisor is a tough decision. Where do you turn?

There are five main issues to consider in selecting an advisor:

1. Objectivity and compensation structure.
2. Professional skills and credentials.
3. Honesty and integrity.
4. Cost.
5. Chemistry.

In this chapter I discuss each factor. My discussion is largely from the vantage point of selecting a Certified Financial Planner (CFP)—that's what I am, it's what I know best, and, frankly, it's what I believe is the best choice for individual investors. But these principles can also be applied to hiring a broker or any other financial advisory professional.

> ### *Hayden Play:*
> ### Be professional or get a professional.
>
> If you measure up to the task of doing it yourself and you have the time, talent, and temperament to pull it off—that's great. If you don't, find a professional advisor who understands and can work with your resources, goals, and value system. Make sure your coach is giving you effective, honest, and objective plays to run with. It's your team and your game.

Objectivity and Compensation Structure

So often when a prospective client comes into my office, I see a portfolio full of funds with lame long-term performance records, performances that had been awful even before the clients bought the funds. What could possibly have compelled an advisor to put this person into these investments? The answer, I believe, is frequently clear: advisor incentives.

Whether it's an extra high sales fee ("load") or a bonus for selling "house" funds, the investment business has, in some instances, motivated salespeople to move products for the wrong reasons. Their interests are not always aligned with your interests.

That's why it's important to seek out objective advice. Objective advice is not always good advice. Unobjective advice isn't necessarily

> ### *Tip:*
> ### *Shop Around*
>
> Before retaining a financial planner, get the names of at least three Certified Financial Planners in your area and interview them with the five factors on page 216 in mind. Any good planner should be willing to give you an introductory, complimentary consultation. You can get referrals for CFPs in your area from the Financial Planning Association, 800-647-6340. To order a financial planning resource kit, call 888-237-6275.

bad advice. But you could raise the odds that the advice you get will be in your interests when those interests and your advisor's interests are aligned.

To figure out how objective or conflicted a potential advisor is, it's helpful to review a bit about the lucrative and not always consumer friendly business of investment and investment advice products. There are three main functions in the financial services business: manufacture of products, distribution, and advice. Things get sticky when one company handles two or three of the functions at the same time. That's when you have to take a hard look at the compensation and motivations of the person advising you and size up whether the advice you're getting is in your best interest.

1. *Manufacturers.* The first function is the manufacture or creation of the products of investments, like mutual funds. In addition to specific investments, these companies may manufacture financial plans as a product for sale. The head of a major brokerage company's financial planning department told me the company would be satisfied just to break even on selling financial plans because the main purpose of the plans was to sell a lot of the company's other investing products. That's not the kind of objective plan or planning you want. Companies that create mutual funds, financial plans, and the like can include banks, insurance firms, mutual fund families, and brokerage houses.

2. *Sales Force/Distributors.* These are the folks who deliver or sell the products or services created by the manufacturer. They are the intermediaries between the manufacturers and the consumers. They are generally paid by the manufacturer in the form of commissions. This group can include full-service stockbrokers and some financial planners. Most distributors offer some kind of advisory service. In many cases, the advice is geared to sell a manufacturer's products. There is either no or very little objectivity—it's an arrangement riddled with conflicts of interest. Many advisor/brokers work for the house and pretend to work for you. When you pick an advisor, you need to rule out this

kind of arrangement. There is no sense in handicapping your game when there are better opportunities.

3. *Advisors.* Finally, we have the advisory services function. This is provided by a range of people, from brokers who offer inexpensive financial plans that are often geared to sell products to independent planners filling a more objective advisory role. You generally want a financial planner who provides advice on a fee basis. The client, not the manufacturer, pays the fee, so the advisor is not beholden to the manufacturer. Generally speaking, you want a Certified Financial Planner (more on that title later).

In weighing the objectivity of a potential advisor, you need to know how a person is positioned with respect to these three functions. Some advisors work for a company that is at once manufacturer, distributor, and advisor. A financial services firm representative, for example, might help you with planning for a fee (advisor) while offering to sell (distribute) a mutual fund created by that firm (manufacturer). As you and others learn more about how these arrangements work, you may start demanding a separation of these services.

The key questions you have to ask to decipher whether an advisor is objective concern how the advisor is compensated and the range of investment options he or she can sell. If a brokerage firm advisor gets paid more for selling a mutual fund produced by that firm than for selling another fund that might be better for your needs, then there could be a conflict of interest and you should walk away.

Or if the firm's house funds are the only option the advisor offers you, either because by the rules there's no other choice or because he or she doesn't bother to research other choices, that's no good, either.

To bring this point home I'll share a personal example. Back in 1971, all of my overhead—including my office and private secretary—was paid by an insurance company because I sold enough of its product to justify it. When I placed my securities registration license with an independent broker/dealer so I could offer a broader range of services and products and not contend with the conflict of the insurance company, I got fired. No more office, secretary, or paid overhead.

Suddenly independent, I decided to do a permanent career disconnect from institutions so that I would not be forced to sell their proprietary products or services. I wanted to be able to pick and choose investments freely, without coercion, pressure, quotas, or misdirected incentives such as fees or even trips. That's when I started charging fees to do planning and money management. Over the years I have kept my securities registration active. Currently I'm with the securities firm of the Financial Network Investment Corporation, a member of the Securities Industry Protection Corporation and a member of ING Advisors Network.

Here's an example of what this change meant. When I was with the insurance company and a client told me she had $100,000 she wanted to keep in cash because it gave her the comfort of security, my first thought was: What can I sell her for that hundred grand that would make a commission? As I started charging fees to manage money, my focus shifted to helping clients create and work objective investment game plans. If they wanted that $100,000 in cash, then that was where it belonged. With fees, the basic idea is that if clients make money, so do I. Conversely, if they lose money, I am paid less. Now the relationships are truly synergistic.

To be sure, there are cases where a person should be paying off credit card, mortgage, or other debt rather than saving and investing. Those moves would not enrich the advisor. You must count on the integrity of the advisor to ensure you are meeting your basic financial needs.

Professional Skills

If you're using an advisor, it's generally because you think there's someone out there who knows what they're doing better than you do in this arena. So skills matter. Skill levels among financial advisors vary wildly. The alphabet soup of registrations and designations they trot out often doesn't offer much clarity. Here are some key factors to look for to make sure your advisor knows what he or she is doing.

First, understand the difference between stockbrokers and financial planners. Full-service stockbrokers can be primarily transaction oriented and will recommend stocks, mutual funds, and other investments and help you put together a portfolio. Online discount brokers also increasingly offer advisory services. Though the onliners rarely go so far as to pick stocks, they might help you create an asset allocation plan, select mutual funds for it, and purchase those funds for you.

When it comes to planners, there are two kinds, Certified Financial Planners (CFPs) and noncertified financial planners. I don't want to totally rule out planners that are not certified, because I know of a few good ones. Many of these are in the process of obtaining their CFPs. But besides a few exceptions, I strongly favor going with a CFP. In fact, former SEC chairman Arthur Levitt has also recommended CFPs.

I favor this route based on personal experience with it. I was enrolled in the first class of CFPs back in 1970. I dropped out because I didn't think it would amount to anything and saw it as just another marketing gimmick. By 1978, I was convinced otherwise, so I completed the requirements and became a CFP that year. I even taught a couple of the courses of the CFP curriculum. Each year the curriculum improved and it got harder for people to get a CFP. In 1985, the CFP Board of Standards was created to help assure the proper ethics, training, and professionalism of CFPs. This board grants the CFP designation and manages a postcertification process. It sets stringent enforcement measures, and many bad apples have lost their licenses. I was on the board of the College for Financial Planning for five years, chairman for two of those. I was also on the CFP Board of Standards for three years (1994 to 1996).

I say all this to assure you that there are extremely bright and ethical people in this profession. Here are the requirements they need to meet to obtain a CFP:

- *Education*. Complete an approved curriculum of six courses, which normally takes anywhere from 18 to 36 months. There are currently about 200 institutions approved to offer these courses.
- *Examination*. Pass a comprehensive 10-hour, two-day examination. Only about 55 percent of the people who have taken this exam have passed it. In the 1990s the CFP Board of Standards provided for a group of financial journalists to take a shorter version of the exam. None of them passed it.

- *Experience.* Work full-time at least three years in this field, that is, in a bank, brokerage, or other financial services operation. The individual is expected to have done counseling, planning, or advisory work with people on a one-on-one basis for compensation.
- *Ethics.* The person must sign and adhere to a professional code of ethics each year. CFPs are also required to complete 30 hours of approved continuing education every two years to keep their licenses.

As of 2002, there were more than 40,000 CFPs in the United States. Licenses have been taken away from about 150 people to date.

In addition to the CFP license, ask the planner about his or her education. The CFP Board of Standards requires a college degree. Ask whether the person has a subspecialty in some area of planning. If so, how does that work? Does the task fall to you to find other experts or will your planner do that, and in that case what are the financial arrangements? Find out if the planner can coordinate with your attorney or CPA when necessary. If the planner manages money, find out how much is under management.

The three years of work experience required to qualify for the CFP license is a good baseline. But I recommend you find someone with five or more years of experience. Planning is an experienced person's game. Veterans will not only have a better feel for the markets, how investing works over the long term, and how to meet the needs of clients, but they'll also have a track record to speak of.

Financial planners don't have standard performance records like mutual fund managers do, because they gear each plan to the needs of a spe-

---

Tip:
Double-Check on Your Planner

If a planner tells you he or she is a licensed CFP and you have any doubt about it, you can check by calling 888-CFP-MARK. For more information check the web site for the CFP Board of Standards, www.cfp-board.org.

cific individual. But you can get a sense of a planner's performance by asking for client references. Request at least three, and ask these clients: Did the planner help the person establish investment goals, and did the investments meet those goals? References are the best way to size up whether a planner has the professional skills this task demands.

Honesty and Integrity

While you're on the phone with those references, ask the planner's current clients about his or her honesty and integrity. By honesty and integrity, I mean not only basic decency—that the person isn't a crook. I also mean candor. If you are with a planner long-term, you're inevitably going to hit on some tough situations—either rough market conditions or your own personal financial stumbles. You want a planner who can be frank about your circumstances and choices. Ask the current clients: Does the planner avoid discussing bad results? Is the person more concerned with his or her own ego than the portfolio? Is the person candid about problems and forthcoming when a change is needed? Remember, you're looking for an advisor, not a salesperson. Honesty and integrity are key to that role. You want someone you can trust.

Cost

There's the old saying that some people know the price of everything and the value of nothing. It's not just the pure fee or the pure performance that matters with a financial planner. It's the value that the planner brings to your total situation. If you're a low-risk investor, the performance of your portfolio established by your planner may not match the S&P 500. But perhaps you're making steady progress toward your goal without incurring the risk the broader market poses. That is a real value conferred by a planner charging a fee.

How much are those fees? Fee-only financial planners generally charge a percentage of assets under management, typically from about 1 percent to 3 percent of assets being managed. Those that charge a percentage generally have a minimum asset requirement ranging from

$100,000 to $500,000. Hourly fees for financial planning can range from $100 to $250.

Some planners and stockbrokers still work on a commission basis from products they sell. The commissions generally range from 2 to 6 percent of the amount being invested.

What do you do if don't have enough money to get a financial planner to take you on? There are several ways to get per-session help. First there are the planners who charge by the hour. Next, discount brokers increasingly are offering advice on asset allocation out of their branches or over the phones. These brokers, like Schwab and Fidelity, have computer programs that generate plans tailored to your needs, based on a series of informational inputs (your age, income, etc.). These advisory services are often available for free or for a minimal fee.

The main downside of per-session help is that the resource delivering it has no stake in or ongoing responsibility for your investments. With per-session advice, the monitoring task falls to you. But if you can't afford to pay someone to manage your money, then hourly sessions or the discount brokers offer a viable alternative. Just take the person's card and try to remember to go back for a checkup on a quarterly basis.

Chemistry

Personal chemistry isn't enough reason to hire someone. In fact, sometimes if you're too friendly with a person, that can affect your ability to evaluate just how strong an advisor the person is. But chemistry is a necessary criterion. Even if all the other factors align—objectivity, professional skills, honesty and integrity, and cost—you must have chemistry with an advisor for the relationship to work.

Chemistry is important for any successful personal or professional relationship. But it's critical with your advisor because it's your money. Even though you might not want to be responsible for your investments on a daily basis, you've got to have a comfort level with the person who is. If you need to confide fears, calm jitters, express disappointment with results, it's not going to work if you're intimidated by the advisor or put off.

What does chemistry mean exactly? Most of all, you need to be sure your advisor listens to you. Pay close attention in the initial session: Is the advisor doing more talking or more listening? Is he or she respecting your desires or trying to talk you out of them? Is he or she promoting an off-the-shelf plan or one that will work for your particular needs? Is he or she trying to understand your values and priorities?

How often does the advisor propose to meet with you? When I establish a relationship with a client, I want to meet at least quarterly, ideally in person. After the first year, when we're in a rhythm and have built up some mutual understanding, meetings can be twice a year. But no less often than that. Finally, I want clients to meet my staff. Ask your advisor to introduce you to the other people in the office you'll be working with—you want to have comfortable relationships with those people, too.

SOS!: Summing Up

Nearly anyone can profit from good advice. But to enjoy the fruits of good advice, you need to make a conscious choice to seek out a worthy advisor. Don't just go with a friend. Don't just rely on one recommendation. I suggest you use a CFP but don't plunge ahead without interviewing a few people first. Once you select someone, the responsibility for day-to-day decisions will be theirs. But the hiring, monitoring, and, if need be, firing responsibilities are yours. Take them seriously and it can pay off.

Epilogue

Money is never my client. Real people are. That's who I wrote this book for: you. I hope it helps you to get a game plan, to work it, and to win it. But most of all, I hope it gives you three things to feel good about:

1. Feel good about making and keeping a commitment. It is a great achievement to take the steps toward crafting your own game plan and to stay your own course. Market movements and sales pitches will inevitably threaten to distract you, to challenge your values. Your commitment to your game plan is your commitment to your beliefs. Take satisfaction and pride in the way you maintain your commitment to yourself.

2. Feel good about how your game plan affects the quality of your life. Ultimately a game plan isn't just about crunching numbers or analyzing mutual funds. It's about creating the means by which you can provide for yourself, for your loved ones, and for the endeavors in life that are meaningful to you.

3. Feel good about helping yourself financially. It requires self-respect to understand that you deserve a game plan and the financial stability and wealth that it can foster. In developing a game plan, you've employed your feelings, your intelligence, and your values in service to yourself. That's a wonderful and worthy accomplishment, one that will help position you financially and emotionally to fulfill all the potential you hold.

My hopes are your hopes.

Notes

Chapter 1 Get the Game Plan Mind-Set—Commitment, Consistency, Courage

1. Belsky, Gary, & Thomas Gilovich. *Why Smart People Make Big Money Mistakes—and How to Correct Them*. New York: Simon & Schuster, 1999, pp. 60–61.
2. Adapted from Zweig, Jason. "Are You Wired for Wealth?" *Money*, October 2002.

Chapter 3 Know Your Goals

1. Loomis, Carol. "Warren Buffet on the Stock Market," *Fortune*, December 10, 2001, www.fortune.com.
2. InvestorGuide University. "What Is Investing?" www.investorguide/com.

Chapter 4 Get the Fund Fever

1. Safire, William, and Leonard Safir. *Good Advice*. New York: Time Books, 1982, p. 332.
2. Graham, Benjamin, and David Dodd. *Security Analysis. 5th ed.* New York: McGraw-Hill, 1988, p. 41.

Chapter 8 Get to Know the Players

1. Rynecki, David. "The Bond King," *Fortune*, March 4, 2002, pp. 98–107.

Index